Desserts

from an

Herb Garden

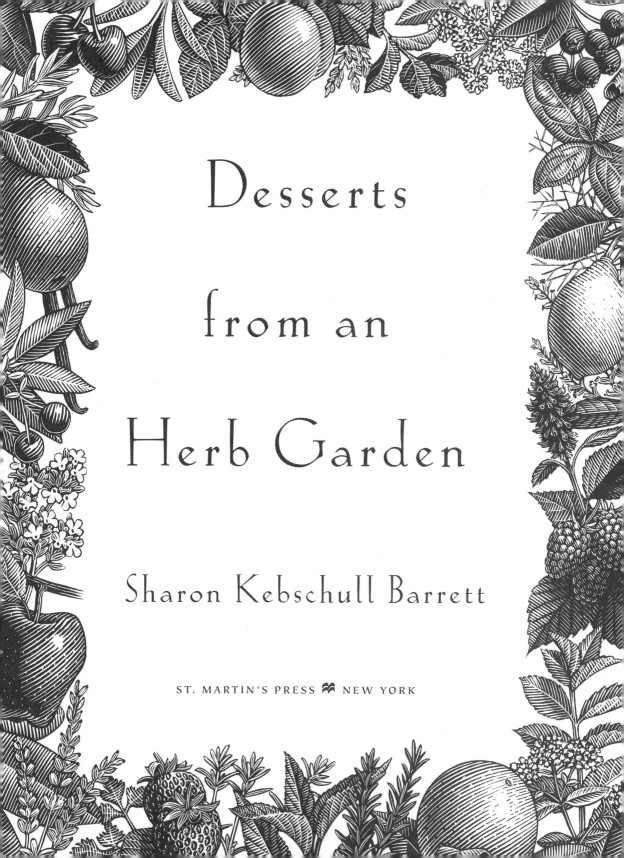

Desserts

from an

Herb Garden

Sharon Kebschull Barrett

ST. MARTIN'S PRESS ✦ NEW YORK

Book design by Gretchen Achilles

Illustrations copyright © 1999 by Elizabeth Traynor

Library of Congress Cataloging-in-Publication Data

Barrett, Sharon Kebschull.
    Desserts from an herb garden : glorious endings with flavors from angelica and
rosemary to lavender and thyme / Sharon Kebshull Barrett.
        p. cm.
    ISBN 0-312-20581-3
    1. Desserts. 2. Cookery (Herbs). I. Title.
TX773.B368 1999
641.8'6—dc21   99-20258
                                                                                    CIP

First Edition: June 1999

10 9 8 7 6 5 4 3 2 1

For James,

with love

Contents

Acknowledgments

I am truly blessed to be part of a loving and helpful family; my husband, parents, sister, and brother-in-law all had much to do with getting this book to this point. First, endless thanks to my husband, James; his willingness to let me leave him temporarily for cooking school started all this, and his love and support ever since through my writing and catering have been amazing and invaluable. Likewise, the constant love and support from my parents, Harv and Georgia Kebschull—especially in getting me to attend a publishing workshop—finally gave me the kick I needed to find an agent and get a book on paper. My mother, who passed along a rich heritage of German food from both sides of the family, can truly take credit for my food career; my father, with his always-firm belief in my future as a journalist, can take credit for my writing. I can't say enough about how much they mean to me. And although we hated it at the time, my competitiveness with my sister, Kim Kebschull Otten, for time in the kitchen also spurred my journey to a food career. She is a truly wonderful cook; the best, most patient sister and friend anyone could ever ask for; a top-notch recipe tester (and indexer); and the person I turn to most for food advice and consultation. And her husband, Mark, is my source for excellent ideas for book titles—no small matter, as it turns out!

Many thanks also go to my agent, Angela Miller, for her cheerful patience and persistence in guiding and representing me; and to Marian Lizzi, a dream of an editor—I still can't believe how easy it has been to work with her. Thanks also to designers Krista Olson and Gretchen Achilles for the beauty of this book; and from way back, thanks to Mark Bittman, who gave me my start in food writing.

Introduction

I never knew oregano was such a popular herb, but invariably "Oregano in desserts?" is the reaction I get when I tell people what my book is about. No, it's not that weird—no oregano in this book, just sweet herbs that add flair to common flavors.

I got started with sweet herbs through my baking catering business, Dessert First. In the beginning, pineapple sage was about as exotic an herb as I used, and then only for garnish. Meanwhile, I was putting my favorites, rosemary and basil, into nearly every dinner I cooked. After one fabulous attempt at combining rosemary and lemon in a cake, the light finally dawned: Why wasn't I trying herbs in more of my desserts?

After all, herbs give a punch to my desserts I can't get in any other way, adding another dimension, another layer of interest.

From lemon and rosemary, I moved to basil with blueberries. Success led me to tarragon with chocolate, lemon balm wherever I used to use lemon zest, sage and thyme with apples, mint in all its forms with chocolate and fruit, and lavender with cherries.

These combinations aren't as unusual as they may first sound. In many of the desserts it is impossible to identify the herb used; especially with the more unusual herbs, I've aimed for a subtle flavor that enhances the dessert. With the exception of mint, to which our palates are accustomed in strong doses, I don't care for food that screams basil or thyme, so you won't find that here. Instead, this is food with interesting flavors that step out of the ordinary but shy away from the bizarre. And it's food that's rapidly becoming popular in restaurants. As pastry chefs look for bold flavors to match the rest of the meal, they're turning to herbs for both fancy and down-home desserts. A famous French chef combines basil with strawberries, while locally, I've seen rosemary in a sweet biscuit topped with cooked apples.

As you'll see from the recipes, my tastes run all over the map. I love complex, architectural desserts in high-end restaurants. I also love homely cobblers and my mother's lemon meringue pie, which starts with a box of pudding. This book reflects all my tastes, from a simple sorbet based on a bag of frozen fruit, to a four-ingredient shortbread, to a spectacular napoleon of white chocolate, lavender, and blueberries.

Simple or sophisticated, time-consuming or quick—there should be something here for whatever mood strikes you.

And if you don't have a garden overflowing with herbs, you'll still find a lot here you can make. Those who find themselves a bit shy about putting herbs into their baking could start with the desserts made with mint; it's a safe way to open your palate to sweet herbs. From there, try desserts with basil, tarragon, rosemary, or thyme—all herbs that are now available in many grocery stores, or easy to grow in a small window pot.

Once you've tried a few of these, you may find your window garden expanding, as you plant all the specialized sweet herbs out there. And before you know it, friends will be asking *you* the oregano question. But don't worry about scaring them off—they'll soon consider you a baker with amazing gifts. And if you do worry, you can always keep secret which herb you've tried today. With these recipes, ignorance will truly be bliss.

Recipes Listed by Herb

Desserts

from an

Herb Garden

Dessert Herbs

and Other

Ingredients

NOTES FROM A DESSERT-HERB GARDENER

Because we live in a solar house, which requires full shade in summer, there are few sunny spots right by any door. This has forced me to plant vegetables down the hill by the street; I try to surround them with flowers so the garden doesn't look quite so ragged, especially in late summer. Over time, though, my herbs have begun taking over the space; while I'd like a few more tomatoes, the herbs have made my garden grow prettier each year.

That rampant growth, although constantly stymied by my cuttings, has proved to me the wisdom of growing herbs in good soil. Many garden books talk about how herbs will thrive anywhere, even in poor soil. With few exceptions, my experience has proved otherwise. Herbs grow best in a good, loose soil. For me, this meant adding some bags of compost and humus to my clay soil before I planted anything, digging in what mulch has broken down each year, and adding more mulch routinely.

Super-rich soil is rarely necessary (and may produce plants with less flavor), but if you're having trouble growing herbs, try pots filled with a high-quality potting soil (such a pot provided me with some of the best basil I've ever grown, in the one sunny spot near my back door). As a bonus, you can bring those pots indoors to have fresh herbs through the winter. The caveat: The herbs I grow indoors taste much milder than those in my garden, a function of either the very rich potting soil or the lack of heat. That's why I always taste my herbs before I use them to judge their strength (after you do this for a while, you'll really begin to notice the differences). They often taste strongest outdoors and later in summer, weakest indoors. I usually double the amount called for when using herbs from indoor pots.

In general, you'll want to grow herbs in good soil that is very well-drained, on the alkaline (sweet) side (I dust with a fair amount of lime each year to counteract my acidic soil), usually in full sun to part shade. Use them often for better flavor and vigorous growth. If you're not cutting them often, you'll still need to pinch back any flowers that develop on annuals to keep them growing. Water them in the morning, not at night, so you don't encourage rot.

I use a few pots by my back door to keep several frequently used herbs close at hand; I also grow a few indoors in the winter, but they'll never be as lush as those outdoors. Still, they're great to have; just give them full sun and keep an eye out in dry houses for the onset of bugs.

Most herbs are easy to start from seed, but I admit to buying nearly all mine as small plants, for instant gratification, and because I would rarely need the amount of plants one seed packet would provide—I'd rather, in my limited space, have all the variety I can fit. At the end of the book I've given a few mail-order sources for extremely hard-to-find plants, but I've found all the rest easily in my local nurseries.

HERBS USED IN THIS BOOK

Except for lavender, all the herbs in this book are used fresh. Dried herbs lack the flavor these desserts need and would too often throw off the texture or proportions. Please don't try to substitute; you'll be disappointed.

But that doesn't mean you need to be a master gardener: Grocery stores now carry many of my garden's must-have herbs—basil, mint, rosemary, sage, tarragon, and thyme—as well as cilantro, fennel, and marjoram.

If you do like to garden, though, you may soon find your herb garden bursting at the seams. It seems that each time I go to a new nursery, I come across another herb variation I haven't yet tried (the mint possibilities alone seem endless). If you're tempted to experiment with new herbs, try substituting similar ones—such as chocolate mint for peppermint—to start. I really enjoy such experimentation, but different herbs may have such different strengths that it can get frustrating if you're not prepared to give it a few tries.

ALLSPICE *Pimenta dioica*: It's not really an herb, but fresh allspice is too good to resist. I saw an article that mentioned growing an allspice tree for its leaves, instead of the berries, and I immediately ordered one. The flavor is wonderful—like the berries but more mellow—and the plant is easy to grow, at least in hot Southern climates, in a pot, in full sun with rich soil. It must come indoors for the winter.

ANGELICA *Angelica archangelica*: Angelica's height—up to 6 feet, though mine has never come near that—and large leaves make it useful as the center plant for my garden's loosely defined herb wheel (which keeps acquiring spokes as I buy new herbs). Use its leaves whenever you're working with a tart fruit; while it has a strong flavor on its own, angelica makes the fruit (or rhubarb, technically a vegetable) taste sweeter, so you'll need less sugar. Herb books often talk about using candied angelica stems in cakes and tarts, but the leaves work so well, why bother? It's a hardy biennial; grow it in rich, moist soil on the acidic side, in sun or part shade. It grows much better in cool climates (mine is in the sun, so with the heat, it generally gives up by August).

ANISE HYSSOP *Agastache foeniculum:* Lots of herbs are described as having an anise or licorice flavor, including anise, a different (and harder to grow) plant. I think anise hyssop, along with tarragon, offers the best licorice flavor. A perennial, it grows to 3 feet high with lavender-blue flower spikes. Grow it in full or part sun; expect it to self-sow. Don't confuse it with regular hyssop, an herb with bitter leaves that I rarely use.

BASIL *Ocimum basilicum:* Easy to grow, and easy to use as fast as it grows, basil is definitely a must-have. I prefer the common (Italian) sweet basil with its large leaves that are easier to strip than globe basils; also look for lemon basil, lime basil, and cinnamon basil, whose flavors truly live up to their names. Lime and cinnamon basil grow like weeds. Lemon basil can be annoying to grow as it needs more pampering, with small, delicate leaves that droop easily and flowers that constantly need to be removed; look for Thai lemon basil, which may be a bit easier to grow. Basil's sweetly spicy flavor works especially well with blueberries and strawberries. It's an annual, easily grown from seed or cuttings; plant it in full sun in good, slightly sweet, moist soil; I often add lime to mine. Basil likes the heat and can't tolerate any frost.

BAY *Laurus nobilis:* Take a whiff of a fresh bay leaf and you'll never go back to the dry ones. The scent and flavor are balanced, more nuanced, and less bitter in the fresh leaves. Be sure you get true bay, not trees marked as California bay, and grow it in full sun (in hot climates, afternoon shade is good) in good, well-drained soil. Except in the Deep South, grow it in a pot to bring indoors for the winter. If you must use dried leaves, use half the amount of fresh required. Health food/gourmet shops have begun carrying fresh leaves.

CILANTRO *Coriandrum sativum:* This herb is hard to grow in my hot, humid summers, but worth it in spring and fall while it lasts. Cilantro has a soapy flavor you either love or despise (I used to despise it; now I crave it). The leaves are hard to match with a dessert flavor, but try the peach cobbler to see the possibilities—just keep the quantities small. Cilantro is an annual that needs full sun or part shade and average, well-drained soil.

FENNEL *Foeniculum vulgare:* Fennel leaves have a delicate, sweet anise flavor that I enjoy, although some of the other anise-flavored herbs may be easier to work with than these feathery leaves. Grow it in full sun in moist, somewhat rich soil; don't let it flower unless you want the seeds. There are three kinds of fennels, any of which can be harvested for the leaves. Florence fennel is the annual that makes the bulb that is eaten (try braising it); the other varieties, a green-leaf fennel and a bronze-leaf one, are perennials that may not live more than a few years but which do self-sow.

LAVENDER *Lavandula angustifolio:* Although I keep reading how easy growing lavender is, I have had very little luck with it in my humid summers. Dried lavender flowers are becoming easier to find in specialty/health-food groceries as lavender grows more popular in both food and perfumes and lotions. Lavender leaves and flowers go gloriously with white chocolate, with pine nuts, and with many kinds of fruit; the Lavender Plum Kuchen included in this book is one of my favorite recipes. A perennial that grows to about 2 feet tall, lavender needs full sun and average, alkaline soil with very good drainage, and can withstand drought once established. *Lavandula angustifolia* is also called English lavender; *Lavandula dentata*, or French lavender, is also good but must be brought indoors in winter. *Lavandula stoechas*, or Spanish lavender, may do better in humid areas and may over-winter.

LEMON BALM and LIME BALM *Melissa officinalis:* While I've become more partial to lemon verbena and lime basil, these two herbs are very useful to have, especially since, at least in my garden, they grow quite fast. With frequent cutting, they make a nice mound about 2 feet tall; should they suffer from neglect, cut them way back—they'll recover nicely. Give them full or part sun (they can even take shade) with average to rich, moist soil; they're hardy perennials that look better if you keep the flowers pinched back (and they self-sow freely, another good reason to keep them under control). Both balms are sweet but slightly medicinal in flavor.

LEMON VERBENA *Aloysia triphylla:* Lemon verbena is my favorite lemon herb, although I have found it a slow grower. A tender perennial, it can grow as high as 10 feet; I've read descriptions of it that call it unattractive, but I once saw one trained as a small tree that was simply beautiful—and the scent was amazing. Mine usually looks more like a very small bush because I cut it back so often. It will lose its leaves with any frost, and can only stand temperatures down to about 25 degrees, so I dig mine up and bring it in for the winter (where I let it go dormant in a cool, dark space). Give it full sun with good, well-drained soil with steady moisture.

MARJORAM *Origanum majorana:* Although its flavor is somewhat like thyme, sweet marjoram is a tougher herb to pair with desserts. It does show up in one delicious recipe in this book—in small amounts, it adds a subtle, haunting flavor. It's a tender perennial that prefers full sun or part shade, in good, well-drained, alkaline soil; grow it as an annual or try bringing it indoors for the winter. It does better in hot, dry areas, but I've been able to grow enough in North Carolina humidity for my needs without any trouble. You may see another herb labeled hardy sweet marjoram, or Italian oregano (*O. x majoricum*), but it's not as sweet.

MINT *Mentha:* If you think you can't grow anything, plant some mint. This invasive, fast-growing herb always makes me feel like a success. I'm sure there are dozens of mints I've never heard of; I prefer basic peppermint and spearmint, chocolate mint, lemon mint, orange mint, pineapple mint, and the hard-to-find banana mint. Apple mint is quite common; I find it very mild and not particularly tasty. Some others, such as ginger mint and grapefruit mint, have had very little flavor when I've grown them. But mint is so easy to grow that it's worth trying all that I find. Experiment with them to see which flavors you prefer. A perennial, mint grows to about 3 feet high—but the problem is the width, not the height. Mint spreads by runners underground, so I often find it sticking up in my garden far from the original plant. It does help to cut the bottom out of its pot, then sink the pot into the ground to contain it a bit, but it still spreads. However, it's easy to pull up and worth growing. Plant it in part shade, although full sun is OK. It likes rich, moist soil, but will tolerate average soil. Cut it nearly to the ground if you need a lot (or as winter arrives); it will grow right back.

ROSEMARY *Rosmarinus officinalis:* The combination of rosemary and lemon is what got me started on this book; I can think of few more perfect matches. Along with basil, I think I could live on anything flavored with rosemary. But much as I like rosemary-roasted potatoes and rosemary-roasted pork, I think I may like it even more in sweet dishes, where it comes as such a pleasant surprise. Around Charleston, South Carolina, where my sister lives, gorgeous 6-foot rosemary shrubs are common. People in colder climates will need to grow it in a pot, to come indoors for the winter. Grow it in full sun in well-drained, slightly alkaline soil. Also try creeping rosemary along borders, beautiful when in flower.

SAGE and PINEAPPLE SAGE *Salvia officinalis* and *Salvia elegans:* Sage has a strong, slightly musty flavor and scent that wouldn't at first seem suited to desserts. Stronger winter fruits, though, such as apples, readily take to sage. Pineapple sage has a good flavor in fruit salads, but I've found it less useful in desserts; the flavor cooks out when heated, and even when it's used cold, I find its flavor less interesting than pineapple mint. I still grow it, though, for its beauty (a great garnish) and its use in salads and sherbet. Grow sage in full sun in well-drained, average, alkaline soil; it's a perennial that doesn't always like my summer humidity, so some years it comes back better than others. You may also find citrus sage (*S. dorisiana);* I find it useful in the same things as pineapple sage.

SUMMER SAVORY and WINTER SAVORY *Satureja hortensis* and *Satureja montana:* Summer savory is an annual, while winter savory—my preference for growing—is an evergreen perennial. Summer savory has a more delicate flavor, but if you keep cutting winter savory, it will produce new growth that has an equally delicate flavor—I try to use the leaves that haven't yet turned tough. Both are usually described as tasting something like thyme with a bite, but I find them more akin to rosemary. Winter savory grows low and spreads; summer savory grows to about a foot and then, at least in my climate, flops over and looks distressed at the heat. Winter savory needs full sun and well-drained, average to poor soil (it likes dry, sandy soil); summer savory needs full sun and light, somewhat rich soil (it will tolerate an average soil).

TARRAGON *Artemesia dracunculus:* Another must-have, and a flavor I find myself craving, tarragon is easy to grow and combines well with so many desserts. Be sure to buy French tarragon—which comes as plants only, not seeds—and skip any flavorless Russian tarragon you see. French tarragon is a 3-foot perennial that needs full sun to part shade in a very well-drained, rich alkaline soil (it will tolerate sandy soils); it also grows well in a pot. Mulch it well in winter.

THYME and LEMON THYME *Thymus vulgaris* and *Thymus citriodorus:* An indispensable herb, and one that goes surprisingly well in many desserts, thyme is the final must-have, in all its forms. I keep seeing new thymes, such as a lavender variation, at herb farms, which are fun to try, but the two essentials are regular thyme and lemon thyme. Give it full sun to part shade and average, well-drained soil; mulch it in winter and cut it back each spring for new growth. It also grows well in containers, so long as you don't water it too much. Make sure you buy common thyme that grows in a small, evergreen, upright shrub—most creeping thymes are too difficult to harvest and strip, although I have two thyme plants that are labeled as creeping thymes that actually have larger-than-usual leaves, making them my favorite thymes.

HARVESTING AND USING HERBS

In general, herbs taste best when cut just before flowering, in the morning after the dew has dried. That's the rule. I rarely follow it. I cut my herbs whenever I need them, and they taste fine. More important than when you cut is how you cut: Never cut back more than a third to half of the plant, and cut whole stems, not just a few leaves off the tops.

If your herbs are dirty, plunge them into a bowl of cold water, swish them around a bit, and let them stand for a few minutes. The grit will drop to the bottom; lift out the herbs and dry them thoroughly—easiest in a salad spinner, OK in paper towels.

To strip small leaves from the stems, hold a stem in one hand at the very top. With the thumb and index finger of your other hand, grasp the stem at the top and run your fingers down the stem—the leaves will strip right off. With large leaves such as basil, however, I generally pluck off groups of leaves just above the stem.

Almost all the recipes in this book use minced herbs. They need to be finely minced, so you don't get a big piece of a leaf in any bite. Pile the leaves on your cutting board; they should be very dry, or you'll end up with mush. Hold a chef's knife by the top of the handle, gripping the top of the base of the blade between your thumb and index finger for control. Place your other hand gently on top of the blade for more control and weight. Without ever lifting the tip of the knife from the board, use a rocking motion to chop the herbs until they are in very small pieces—almost to a dust.

There are three standard ways to get herb flavor into a dessert. You can mix minced or whole herbs in with hot or melting ingredients to bring out their oils (especially useful if you want to strain out the herb to avoid its texture), or toss the minced herbs with the dry ingredients (be sure the herb is evenly distributed throughout the flour, without clumps, or the flavor won't be right). If you would rather not mince the herbs, you can, in many recipes, grind the whole leaves with some or all of the sugar. A few of the recipes must be made this way, to bring out enough of the herb's flavor. In other cases, you would not want to grind the herbs because it would give too strong a flavor or create an unpleasant color. But in most cases, it's fine; use your judgment, based on whether the color will show and how strong the herb is to start (I would probably not, for example, do this with sage in desserts). To translate the amounts, use twice as many whole leaves, packed, as the amount of minced herb called for (so 2 tablespoons minced herbs translates to ¼ packed cup, which is 4 tablespoons, whole herb leaves).

NOTE: Unless the recipe says otherwise, measure your minced herbs by very lightly pressing them into a measuring spoon or cup—do not pack them down.

INGREDIENTS AND HINTS

🌿 BUTTER: Unsalted butter is best in any kind of cooking, but it's crucial in baking. It lets you control the amount of salt overall, and generally, unsalted butter will be fresher than salted. Salt acts as a preservative and can cover up off-flavors or rancidity, so salted butter can stay on the shelf longer. Avoid it.

🌿 EGGS: All eggs in these desserts should be Grade A large eggs.

🌿 CREAM: I use a lot of cream in my desserts, as I prefer richness to sweetness. If you can find (and afford) it, look for cream that has been only pasteurized, not ultra-pasteurized. It will whip like a dream (even by hand, it's very quick) and have a fresher flavor, as it has not been taken to the high temperature that ultra-pasteurization requires. Look for it in health-food or gourmet stores. And try to buy heavy cream, not whipping cream, which has a lower butterfat content.

🌿 FLOUR: The recipes use either all-purpose or cake flour. When necessary, I have specified a preference for unbleached or bleached all-purpose flour; in general I prefer unbleached, but since bleached flour is slightly softer, it's a better choice for some tender cookies and pastries. If you can't get unbleached, bleached will do in all cases. And if you have a soft, Southern flour, such as White Lily, on hand, you may use that in place of cake flour where noted—it's virtually as soft as cake flour.

🌿 MILK: Unless the recipe specifies, you may use any milk you like—whole, 2 percent, or skim. I drink skim milk, so it's what I bake with when at all possible.

🌿 SALT: Please make the effort to search out boxes of coarse (kosher) salt; in some supermarkets it's kept with ethnic ingredients. This, not table salt, is what I use in all my cooking and baking, except for a few times when I prefer the flavor of sea salt. Many chefs prefer coarse salt for its cleaner flavor and the ability to feel the grains between your fingers when you're tossing some into a dish. I strongly recommend cooking with it, but if you prefer to stick with table salt, you'll need to use about ⅓ less than the coarse salt called for.

🌿 TURBINADO SUGAR: I like sprinkling turbinado on top of pie crusts; the sugar doesn't melt during baking, giving a more decorative crust. It's a pale, raw sugar; if you can't find it or Demerara, another raw sugar, use granulated sugar or granulated brown sugar instead.

🌿 CHOCOLATE: For the recipes in this book, use the best quality chocolate you can find—but if you can, buy that chocolate as chocolate chips. Several good brands of chocolate now come in chips, and while they aren't always the best choice, they work fine for these recipes and save you the time and hassle of chopping chocolate, one of my least-favorite chores. The key is that they be high-quality chips, such as Guittard or Ghirardelli, or the recipes will disappoint.

Finally, a few random hints that will make these recipes easier and neater:

🌿 When I make drop cookies, I use a small scoop that looks like a mini ice cream scoop. It makes cookie-making faster and gives even cookies—worth the small cost.

🌿 Whenever I'm using a mixer to beat an ingredient that splatters, especially whipping cream, I drape a towel over the top of the mixer so that it hangs down over the outer edge of the bowl. This catches the splatters quite well.

🌿 Instead of calling for greased cookie sheets, all the recipes in this book use parchment paper. I use parchment paper constantly, to save clean-up time and to guarantee my food will lift off the cookie sheet without fail. Many kitchen shops and gourmet stores sell the paper in rolls, but I dislike buying it that way and find it expensive. To get it in sheets, order it from one of the sources listed at the back of the book. If you don't want to use parchment paper, lightly grease the sheets instead.

Cookies

and

Candies

Mint Julep Truffles

I've never been thrilled with truffles that are rolled in cocoa; I dislike having the residue of that dry powder on my tongue. Rolling truffles in chocolate shavings instead gives a wonderful texture contrast to the creamy interiors. For authenticity, use "Kentucky Colonel" mint.

1. Place chopped chocolate in a mixing bowl and set aside. Heat cream and mint leaves in a small pan to a simmer; remove from heat and pour over chocolate. Stir in butter and bourbon; whisk until chocolate is melted and smooth. Cover chocolate mixture with plastic wrap (press wrap onto surface of chocolate) and chill for two hours, or until firm.

2. Put chocolate shavings in a shallow bowl or pie tin. Using a very small cookie scoop, a melon baller, or a teaspoon, scoop out balls of chilled chocolate, rounding them quickly between your palms if necessary. Drop balls into shavings and roll quickly to cover. Store in an airtight container in refrigerator 1 to 2 weeks.

2 DOZEN TRUFFLES

6 ounces bittersweet or semisweet chocolate, chopped (1 cup chips)

⅓ cup heavy cream

1 tablespoon minced mint leaves

2 tablespoons unsalted butter, very soft

1 tablespoon bourbon

About 2 ounces bittersweet or semisweet chocolate, shaved with a vegetable peeler

Sambuca Cookies

These are buttery, tender cookies based on a foolproof recipe from *Cook's Illustrated* magazine. They can be made either singly or sandwiched. If you don't sandwich the cookies, the recipe can easily be cut in half.

2 ½ cups bleached all-purpose flour

¼ cup cornstarch

2 teaspoons baking powder

⅛ teaspoon coarse salt

1 ½ tablespoons chopped tarragon leaves

1 cup granulated sugar

¾ cup (1 ½ sticks) unsalted butter, softened

¼ cup vegetable shortening

2 egg yolks

3 tablespoons half-and-half

2 teaspoons vanilla extract

GANACHE GLAZE

½ cup heavy cream

1 tablespoon instant espresso powder

6 ounces (1 cup) semisweet or bittersweet chocolate chips

1. Preheat oven to 350 degrees.

2. Whisk together flour, cornstarch, baking powder, salt, and tarragon leaves; set aside. In a large bowl, beat sugar, butter, and vegetable shortening on high speed until light and fluffy. Scrape down sides of bowl with a spatula and add egg yolks, half-and-half, and vanilla; beat until combined well. With mixer running, slowly add flour mixture until combined.

3. With your hands, press dough together in bowl. Depending on the size of your rolling surface, roll out a quarter to half of the dough at a time on a floured surface, to about ¼-inch thick. Cut dough into 2-inch rounds with a floured cookie cutter. Place rounds on parchment paper–lined baking sheets. Bake 10 to 12 minutes until golden. Remove to racks and let cool.

4. To make glaze, whisk together cream and espresso powder and bring just to a simmer over medium heat. Remove from heat, add chips, and stir until melted. Dip cookies halfway into glaze and return to parchment-lined sheets to cool and set (or line sheets with waxed paper). Store in an airtight container.

VARIATION: *Sambuca Sandwich Cookies.* Double the chocolate

ganache glaze. Remove half the mixture to a medium mixing bowl and cool until thick, in refrigerator or, quickly, by stirring over a bowl of iced water. With an electric mixer, beat ganache until it is just light and fluffy. Pipe or spread a small dollop of ganache onto the bottoms of half the cookies; top with the remaining cookies. Dip sandwiched cookies halfway into remaining glaze (rewarm glaze if it has thickened) and return to parchment-lined sheets to cool and set.

6 DOZEN COOKIES

Pine Nut–Lavender Brittle

These flavors always make me think of Provence; the pine nuts get lightly toasted during the cooking, and the lavender sends off a powerful burst of scent when you add it. You'll need a candy thermometer to make this unless you're an experienced candy maker.

1 ½ cups sugar

⅓ cup light corn syrup

3 tablespoons water

1 ½ cups pine nuts

1 tablespoon unsalted butter

¾ teaspoon baking soda

½ teaspoon dried lavender flowers

1. Butter your largest cookie sheet, a jellyroll pan, or a marble slab and set aside. Butter a wide rubber spatula and set aside.

2. Mix sugar, corn syrup, and water in a medium saucepan; cook over medium heat, stirring with a wooden spoon, until sugar dissolves. As this is happening, brush down sides of pan with a pastry brush dipped in water to keep crystals from forming. Add pine nuts and your candy thermometer; cook, stirring often to keep nuts from burning, to 300 degrees (hard-crack stage), about 15 minutes.

3. Remove from heat and stir in butter, baking soda, and lavender until butter is melted. Working quickly, pour into the prepared pan and spread evenly with the buttered spatula. Let cool completely at room temperature and break into pieces; it's easiest to do this by lightly dropping the pan on the counter to break into big pieces, and then breaking by hand. Store in an airtight container.

ABOUT 1 ¼ POUNDS BRITTLE

Cinnamon Basil Polenta Cookies

Crisp and crunchy with cornmeal, these simple cookies go well with ice cream or a cup of tea. The cinnamon basil is a nice touch, but any basil could work here.

1. Preheat oven to 350 degrees.

2. Whisk together cornmeal, flour, cornstarch, baking powder, salt, and cinnamon; set aside. In a food processor or blender, whiz cinnamon basil leaves and sugar until leaves are finely ground. Transfer to a medium bowl; add butter and vegetable shortening. Beat on high speed until light and fluffy. Scrape down sides with a spatula and add egg yolk, half-and-half, and vanilla; beat until combined well. With mixer running, slowly add flour mixture until combined.

3. Scoop out heaping teaspoons of dough onto parchment paper–lined baking sheets, placing them 2 inches apart. Bake 10 to 12 minutes, until golden. Remove to racks and let cool; dust with confectioners' sugar before serving or storing, if desired. Store in an airtight container.

3 DOZEN COOKIES

½ cup yellow cornmeal, preferably stone-ground

¾ cup bleached all-purpose flour

2 tablespoons cornstarch

1 teaspoon baking powder

Pinch of coarse salt

¼ teaspoon ground cinnamon

2 tablespoons (packed) whole cinnamon basil leaves

½ cup granulated sugar

6 tablespoons unsalted butter, softened

2 tablespoons vegetable shortening

1 egg yolk

2 tablespoons half-and-half or cream

1 teaspoon vanilla extract

GARNISH

Confectioners' sugar (optional)

Maple Walnut Cookies

Since allspice leaves are definitely not a common ingredient, I didn't want to over-represent them in this book. But I wanted to include one recipe to introduce them. Growing an allspice tree is surprisingly easy, and mincing the leaves creates such a great scent that it's a flavor worth pursuing.

½ cup (1 stick) unsalted butter, softened

⅓ cup pure maple syrup

1 cup chopped walnuts

1 teaspoon vanilla extract

2 teaspoons minced allspice leaves

2 cups all-purpose flour

⅛ teaspoon coarse salt

GARNISH
Confectioners' sugar

1. Preheat oven to 325 degrees.

2. In a medium bowl, beat butter and maple syrup on medium speed until light. Beat in walnuts and vanilla. In a separate bowl, whisk together allspice leaves, flour, and salt; beat into butter mixture just until combined.

3. Scoop heaping teaspoon-size balls of dough close together onto a parchment paper–lined baking sheet, or shape balls into crescents and then place on sheet. Bake 20 minutes, until golden. Cool on a wire rack; dust with confectioners' sugar when cold. Store in an airtight container.

4 DOZEN COOKIES

Orange Sugar Cookies

My mother has a decided preference for small, delicate cookies; she usually makes hers smaller than the recipe says. Ordinarily, I do the same, but these cookies taste like the ones we used to buy when I was little, which seemed wonderfully large. The anise hyssop is only a background flavor here, adding depth.

1. Preheat oven to 375 degrees.

2. With a vegetable peeler, remove strips of zest (top layer of peel) from orange. Place in a food processor or blender with anise hyssop leaves and ¾ cup sugar, and process until leaves and zest are finely ground.

3. Transfer to a large bowl, and add butter and salt. Beat on high speed until light and fluffy. Scrape down sides of bowl with a spatula, and beat in orange extract and egg until blended. On low speed, beat in baking powder and flour just until blended. Dough will be very soft.

4. Scoop out 1-inch balls of dough (if you're not using a cookie scoop, you may want to chill the dough before forming balls). Place them 2 inches apart on a parchment paper–lined baking sheet. Run the bottom of a drinking glass under cold water, then dip in the remaining 2 tablespoons sugar. Use bottom of glass to flatten balls to 2½-inch rounds, dipping glass in sugar before each cookie.

5. Bake cookies for 12 to 15 minutes, reversing sheets from top to bottom and front to back after 6 minutes. Cool on a wire rack; store in an airtight container.

1 small orange

¼ cup (packed) whole anise hyssop leaves

¾ cup plus 2 tablespoons granulated sugar, divided

¾ cup (1 ½ sticks) unsalted butter, softened

½ teaspoon coarse salt

1 teaspoon pure orange extract

1 egg

1 teaspoon baking powder

1 ¾ cups all-purpose flour

2 DOZEN COOKIES

Buttercream-Filled Macaroons

With only three ingredients, macaroons offer a simple but pure flavor, better here dressed up with a chocolate mint or orange mint buttercream. If you don't have a pastry bag, you can scoop out the cookies, but try to flatten them before baking, to make the sandwiches stay flat on a serving platter.

12 ounces (1½ cups) almond paste

½ cup granulated sugar

3 egg whites

1 recipe Chocolate Mint Buttercream (recipe follows)

GARNISH

Confectioners' sugar

1. Preheat oven to 400 degrees.

2. In a large bowl, beat almond paste on low speed until broken up. Beat in granulated sugar until mixture is light. Add egg whites and beat on high speed 2 minutes, until smooth and creamy.

3. Transfer batter to a pastry bag with a large, plain tip. Pipe out in a spiral 1½-inch flat circles about 1 inch apart onto parchment paper–lined baking sheets. Bake 1 sheet at a time on the oven's middle rack for 8 to 10 minutes, until set and barely golden. Remove paper to wire racks and let cookies cool completely. Peel paper off cookies and spread bottoms of half the cookies with buttercream; sandwich with remaining cookies. Dust with confectioners' sugar to serve. Store in an airtight container.

2 DOZEN SANDWICH COOKIES

Chocolate Mint Buttercream

1. Place the chips in a small microwave-proof bowl and cover with plastic wrap. Heat chips on 50 percent power for 1 minute and stir to finish the melting. The chocolate should not be hot.

2. In a small bowl, beat butter on high speed until fluffy. Beat in ¼ cup sugar, then add melted chocolate. Beat in ½ cup sugar, then beat in cream and mint leaves. Beat in remaining ¼ cup sugar until blended well; add more sugar or cream as needed to achieve a spreadable consistency.

VARIATION: *Orange Mint Buttercream.* Omit the chocolate chips. Increase cream to 2 to 3 tablespoons as needed, beating first 2 tablespoons in with the first ¼ cup sugar; substitute 1½ tablespoons minced orange mint leaves for the chocolate mint.

2 ounces (about ¼ cup) semisweet chocolate chips

2 tablespoons unsalted butter, softened

1 cup confectioners' sugar

1 tablespoon heavy cream, or as needed

2 tablespoons minced chocolate mint leaves

Chocolate Mint Biscotti

I make classic, no-butter biscotti that are crisp but not tooth-shattering; my husband doesn't drink coffee, so he likes cookies he doesn't have to dunk first. These follow a basic formula I've seen in a variety of recipes: 2 eggs and 1 cup sugar to 2 cups flour and 1 teaspoon baking powder. From there the flavor variations are endless (as in the two recipes that follow). These biscotti will keep for weeks in an airtight container.

1 cup granulated sugar

¼ cup (packed) whole chocolate mint leaves

2 eggs

1 teaspoon vanilla extract

2 cups all-purpose flour

1 teaspoon baking powder

½ teaspoon coarse salt

6 ounces (1 cup) semisweet chocolate chips

2½ DOZEN BISCOTTI

1. Preheat oven to 350 degrees.

2. Grind sugar and chocolate mint leaves in a food processor for 30 seconds. Transfer to a medium bowl and whisk in eggs and vanilla until blended. In another bowl, whisk together flour, baking powder, and salt. Fold this with chocolate chips into egg mixture with a rubber spatula until incorporated. Dough will be sticky.

3. Divide dough in half. Wet your hands and shake them off, but don't dry them. On a parchment paper–lined baking sheet, press each half into a log that measures about 11 inches long by 2 inches wide; press down on top until the log is ½ inch high. Leave about 2 inches between logs.

4. Bake 30 to 35 minutes, until golden. Remove from oven; lower heat to 325 degrees. Cool pan on a wire rack for 15 minutes. Transfer logs to a cutting board and cut crosswise with a serrated knife into ¾-inch slices. Return slices, standing up, to the parchment-lined baking sheet, spaced slightly apart. Bake 15 minutes more, until crisp. Transfer to racks to cool. Store in an airtight container.

Coconut-Lime Biscotti

Coconut biscotti are among my most popular, and the addition of lime basil (you need a lot to taste it) has made them even better. These are softer and slightly sweeter than some of the other biscotti I make, due to the coconut.

1. Preheat oven to 350 degrees.

2. Grind sugar and lime basil leaves in a food processor for 30 seconds. Transfer to a medium bowl, and whisk in eggs and vanilla until blended. In another bowl, whisk together flour, baking powder, salt, and coconut. Fold into egg mixture with a rubber spatula until incorporated. Dough will be sticky.

3. Divide dough in half. Wet your hands and shake them off, but don't dry them. On a parchment paper–lined baking sheet, press each half into a log that measures 11 inches long by 2 inches wide; press down on top until the log is ½ inch high. Leave about 2 inches between logs.

4. Bake 30 to 35 minutes, until golden. Remove from oven; lower heat to 325 degrees. Cool pan on a wire rack for 15 minutes. Transfer logs to a cutting board and cut crosswise with a serrated knife into ¾-inch slices. Return slices, standing up, to the parchment-lined baking sheet, spaced slightly apart. Bake 15 minutes more, until crisp. Transfer to racks to cool. Store in an airtight container.

2½ DOZEN BISCOTTI

1 cup granulated sugar

½ cup (packed) whole lime basil leaves

2 eggs

½ teaspoon vanilla extract

2 cups all-purpose flour

1 teaspoon baking powder

½ teaspoon coarse salt

¾ cup shredded, sweetened dried coconut

Lemon-Rosemary Biscotti

Once I discovered the glorious combination of lemon and rosemary, I started using it everywhere. Like everything using this combination, these biscotti go well with a cup of tea.

1 cup granulated sugar

2 eggs

1 teaspoon vanilla extract

1 tablespoon minced lemon verbena leaves

2 cups all-purpose flour

1 teaspoon baking powder

½ teaspoon coarse salt

1 teaspoon minced rosemary leaves

1. Preheat oven to 350 degrees.

2. In a medium bowl, whisk together sugar, eggs, vanilla, and lemon verbena leaves until blended. In another bowl, whisk together flour, baking powder, salt, and rosemary leaves. Fold into egg mixture with a rubber spatula until incorporated. Dough will be sticky.

3. Divide dough in half. Wet your hands and shake them off, but don't dry them. On a parchment paper–lined baking sheet, press each half into a log that measures 11 inches long by 2 inches wide; press down on top until the log is ½ inch high. Leave about 2 inches between logs.

4. Bake 30 to 35 minutes, until golden. Remove from oven; lower heat to 325 degrees. Cool pan on a wire rack for 15 minutes. Transfer logs to a cutting board and cut crosswise with a serrated knife into ¾-inch slices. Return slices, standing up, to the parchment-lined baking sheet, spaced slightly apart. Bake 15 minutes more, until crisp. Transfer to racks to cool. Store in an airtight container.

2½ DOZEN BISCOTTI

Triple-Lemon Madeleines

These tender, cakey cookies are based on a recipe I developed for a story in *Cook's Illustrated* magazine; I've simplified the directions a bit and added the herbs for a complex lemon flavor. If you have access to a bleached, soft Southern flour, such as White Lily, you can use ½ cup of it in place of the other flours. These cookies freeze very well.

1. Preheat the oven to 375 degrees. Thoroughly coat a madeleine mold that makes 12 3-inch-long cookies with Baker's Coating (page 38), brushing the rims as well.

2. Whisk together both flours, salt, and all herb leaves. In a medium bowl, beat egg yolks, egg, sugar, and vanilla for about 10 minutes on high speed, until a ribbon falls when you lift the beaters. Gently fold in flour mixture, then the melted butter.

3. Divide the batter among the molds (depending on how fluffy you got the eggs, you may have just a bit of batter left over; fill molds three-quarters full) and bake for 10 to 12 minutes, until the tops are golden and the cakes spring back when pressed lightly. Immediately remove from oven and hold the pan over a dry towel. Tap one long side of the pan against the counter to release the madeleines onto towel; let cool on towel and store in an airtight container.

I DOZEN MADELEINES

¼ cup all-purpose flour

¼ cup cake flour

Pinch of coarse salt

1 teaspoon minced
   lemon thyme leaves

1 teaspoon minced
   lemon verbena leaves

1 teaspoon minced
   lemon balm leaves

2 egg yolks

1 whole egg

¼ cup granulated sugar

1½ teaspoons vanilla

4 tablespoons unsalted
   butter, melted

Apricot-Savory Cookie Cups

These are tender, light cookies brimming with glistening apricot jam; they go wonderfully

with a cup of tea. You could use summer savory instead of winter savory.

¾ cup all-fruit apricot jam (10-ounce jar)

2 teaspoons minced winter savory leaves

1¼ cups bleached all-purpose flour

¼ cup cornstarch

¼ teaspoon coarse salt

4 ounces cream cheese, softened

½ cup (1 stick) unsalted butter, softened

¼ cup confectioners' sugar

1 teaspoon vanilla extract

1. Preheat oven to 350 degrees.

2. In a small bowl, stir together jam and savory leaves; set aside. In a medium bowl, whisk together flour, cornstarch, and salt. In a large bowl, beat cream cheese, butter, and confectioners' sugar on high speed until light and fluffy; beat in vanilla. On low speed, beat in flour mixture until just combined.

3. Divide dough among 24 cups in miniature muffin tins, pressing dough evenly into bottom and up sides. Prick bottoms of cups with a fork. Bake 20 minutes.

4. Remove tins from oven; leave oven on. Divide jam mixture among cups. Bake 10 minutes more, until jam begins to bubble. Cool tins on a wire rack; when cool, remove cookie cups, gently dislodging them with the point of a knife if necessary. Store in an airtight container.

2 DOZEN COOKIES

Lemon Thyme Shortbread

Adding lemon thyme to tender, simple, traditional shortbread takes the flavors up a notch; the buttery, toasted flavor of the cookie takes well to the thyme. Like so many desserts with thyme and rosemary, this tastes great with a cup of tea.

1. Preheat oven to 350 degrees.

2. Whisk lemon thyme leaves, flour, and sugar together. Cut in butter with fingertips until mixture resembles coarse crumbs. Knead dough lightly until it can form a ball. Pat into an 8-inch circle on a parchment paper–lined baking sheet. Press with the tines of a fork around the outer rim to make a decorative edge; then prick with the fork to mark 16 wedges.

3. Bake 30 to 35 minutes, until golden. Cool pan on a wire rack; cut into wedges while barely warm. Store in an airtight container..

16 WEDGES

1 ½ tablespoons minced lemon thyme leaves

1 ½ cups bleached all-purpose flour

⅓ cup granulated sugar

½ cup (1 stick) unsalted butter, cut into 16 pieces

Lemon Balm Bars

Light and lemony, based on a recipe my mother has used for years, these bars are a simple introduction to using herbs in desserts. You can cut them into even smaller bars for a delicate presentation.

CRUST

1 cup bleached all-purpose flour

¼ cup confectioners' sugar

½ cup (1 stick) unsalted butter

FILLING

1 cup granulated sugar

¼ cup (packed) whole lemon balm leaves

2 tablespoons bleached all-purpose flour

½ teaspoon baking powder

Pinch of coarse salt

3 tablespoons fresh lemon juice

2 eggs

GARNISH

Confectioners' sugar

1. Preheat oven to 325 degrees if using a glass or nonstick baking dish, 350 degrees for all other types.

2. Make crust: Stir together flour and sugar. Cut in butter with your fingertips or a pastry blender (or pulse in a food processor—do not overprocess) until mixture resembles coarse crumbs. Press evenly into an 8-inch-square baking pan. Bake for 20 minutes.

3. Meanwhile, make filling: In a food processor or blender, whiz sugar and lemon balm leaves until leaves are finely ground. Transfer to a medium bowl and whisk in flour, baking powder, and salt. Whisk in lemon juice and eggs.

4. As soon as crust is baked, pour filling over and return to oven. Bake 20 to 25 minutes more, until top feels barely firm. Cool on wire rack; dust with confectioners' sugar before cutting. Store in an airtight container.

16 BARS

Tarragon Blueberry Streusel Bars

A licorice undertone to the blueberry filling, tied in with the buttery crust, makes these cookies elegant. You can also bake this in a small tart or springform pan and cut it into wedges to serve.

1. Preheat oven to 375 degrees; grease an 8-inch-square pan.

2. Stir together flour and sugar; cut in butter with your fingertips or a pastry blender until mixture resembles coarse crumbs. Set aside 1 cup of this mixture. With a fork, beat the egg yolk briefly with the vanilla and stir into the remaining flour mixture. Stir until it begins to come together, then press gently with your fingertips until it can almost form a ball. Press into prepared pan.

3. Mix jam with tarragon leaves; spread over crust in pan. Sprinkle reserved flour mixture evenly over top.

4. Bake 40 to 45 minutes, until set and golden. Cool on a wire rack. Dust with confectioners' sugar before serving. Store in an airtight container.

16 BARS

1½ cups all-purpose flour

¼ cup granulated sugar

½ cup (1 stick) cold unsalted butter

1 egg yolk

1 teaspoon vanilla extract

1 cup blueberry jam or preserves

2½ teaspoons minced tarragon leaves

GARNISH

Confectioners' sugar

Chocolate Mint Brownie Sandwiches

Two thin brownie layers sandwiching a chocolatey mint cream make a nice variation, and they're easier to serve and eat than iced brownies. Don't worry if the delicate tops crack a bit in cutting; the confectioners' sugar will hide that.

4 ounces semisweet chocolate, chopped (about ⅔ cup semisweet chips)

2 ounces unsweetened chocolate, chopped

1 cup (2 sticks) unsalted butter

1 cup all-purpose flour

1 teaspoon baking powder

½ teaspoon coarse salt

¼ cup (packed) whole mint leaves

1 cup granulated sugar

3 eggs

1 teaspoon vanilla

1 recipe Chocolate Mint Buttercream or Orange Mint Buttercream (page 23)

GARNISH

Confectioners' sugar

1. Preheat oven to 350 degrees; grease a 10-by-15-inch jellyroll pan.

2. In a medium saucepan, melt both chocolates and butter over medium-low heat. Set aside to cool 5 minutes.

3. In a small bowl, whisk together flour, baking powder, and salt; set aside. In a food processor or blender, grind mint leaves and sugar until leaves are minced. Transfer to a medium bowl and add eggs; beat on high speed for about 3 minutes, until light and fluffy. Beat in chocolate mixture and vanilla. On low speed, beat in flour mixture just until combined.

4. Pour batter into prepared pan. Bake about 20 minutes, until a tester inserted in the middle comes out clean. Cool on a wire rack.

5. Cut into 24 squares. Spread buttercream onto the bottoms of half the squares; top with remaining squares, bottoms facing buttercream. Cut each square into 2 or 4 triangles. Dust with confectioners' sugar to serve. Store in an airtight container.

24 SANDWICHES

Tarragon Fig Bars

I am thrilled with how easy these turned out to be, and how good—a soft, puffy cookie and a tarragon flavor that just comes through at the end of the bite.

1. Snip any large stems off the figs and place them in a small saucepan. Add granulated sugar, water, and tarragon leaves; bring to a boil over medium-high heat. Lower heat and simmer, uncovered, 15 to 25 minutes, or until most of the liquid is absorbed and the figs are softened. Transfer figs and their liquid to a food processor and puree until no lumps remain. Let cool.

2. Preheat oven to 350 degrees, and grease a 9-inch-square baking pan.

3. In a small bowl, whisk together flour, baking powder, and salt. In a medium bowl, beat butter and brown sugar on high speed until light and fluffy. Beat in eggs 1 at a time, beating well after each addition. Beat in vanilla. On low speed, beat in flour mixture just until incorporated.

4. Spread half the dough into the prepared pan. Spread fig filling evenly over dough, spreading to the edges. Drop remaining dough in dollops on the figs and spread gently with a spatula to cover figs completely.

5. Bake 30 minutes, until puffed and golden. Cool on a wire rack, then cut into small bars. Store in an airtight container.

36 SMALL BARS

8 ounces (1½ cups) dried figs, such as Mission figs

¼ cup granulated sugar

¾ cup water

2 tablespoons minced tarragon leaves

1½ cups all-purpose flour

1 teaspoon baking powder

¾ teaspoon coarse salt

½ cup (1 stick) unsalted butter

¾ cup firmly packed light brown sugar

2 eggs

1 teaspoon vanilla extract

Cakes

of All

Kinds

Lemon-Rosemary Cream Cake

Lighter than most since it doesn't call for butter, this cake works well as an afternoon snack or an end to a cool summer dinner—and the leftovers make a great breakfast.

1. Preheat oven to 350 degrees. Grease and flour a 10-cup Bundt pan, or brush pan with Baker's Coating (recipe follows).

2. Whisk together flour, salt, baking powder, and rosemary and lemon verbena leaves; set aside. In a small bowl, whisk together buttermilk and vanilla; set aside. In a large bowl, beat eggs on medium speed with sugar until thick; batter should fall in a ribbon when beaters are lifted. With mixer on low speed or by hand, alternately mix in flour and buttermilk mixtures, beginning and ending with flour. Mix just until combined.

3. In another bowl with clean beaters, beat cream until stiff peaks form; gently fold into batter. Pour batter into prepared pan and smooth the top. Bake for 45 minutes, until the top just springs back when pressed. Cool 10 minutes in the pan on a rack, then turn cake out onto rack to cool completely.

4. Transfer cake to a serving platter and glaze: Whisk together confectioners' sugar, half-and-half, and lemon juice and drizzle over cake.

12 OR 24 SERVINGS

2 cups bleached all-purpose flour

¾ teaspoon coarse salt

1½ teaspoons baking powder

1 teaspoon minced rosemary leaves

1 tablespoon minced lemon verbena or lemon zest

½ cup nonfat or low-fat buttermilk

1 teaspoon vanilla extract

3 eggs

1¼ cups granulated sugar

¾ cup heavy cream

GLAZE

1 cup confectioners' sugar

1 tablespoon half-and-half or milk

4 teaspoons fresh lemon juice

Baker's Coating

Whenever a recipe calls for greasing and flouring pans, use this instead; simply brush it on with a pastry brush. I have had glorious luck since I started using this mixture—I no longer worry about anything sticking. Plus, flour clouds no longer float through the kitchen as I shake flour around a pan. If you bake often, make a double batch. It keeps for months.

1 cup vegetable shortening

1 cup vegetable oil (I use canola oil)

1 cup flour

1. In a medium bowl with an electric mixer, beat shortening, oil, and flour together until smooth (consistency will resemble sour cream). Transfer to an airtight container to store; does not need refrigeration.

2. To use, brush on a thin coating with a pastry brush.

Apple-Basil Cake

Based on a cake that's my mother-in-law's specialty, this is moist, rich, and subtly spiced. The Cinnamon Basil–Apple Ice Cream (page 101) makes a spectacular match.

1. Preheat oven to 325 degrees. Grease a 10-inch removable-bottom tube pan.

2. Sift together the flour, baking soda, and salt. Whisk in basil leaves until thoroughly dispersed in the flour; set aside. In a large bowl, beat together oil and sugar on low speed. On medium speed, add eggs 1 at a time, beating well after each addition. Add vanilla and increase speed to high; beat for 30 seconds. On low speed, add flour mixture and beat just until blended.

3. Fold in apples with a spatula; spread batter in prepared pan. Bake for 1 hour and 15 minutes, until a toothpick inserted in the cake comes out clean.

4. Just before cake is done, make glaze: Over medium heat, melt the butter in a small saucepan and whisk in both sugars, cream, and vanilla. Boil glaze for 1 minute.

5. When the cake comes out of the oven, immediately pour the hot glaze over. Let cake cool completely on a rack before removing from pan. To remove from pan, run a knife around the edge to release it, then run a thin knife between cake and pan bottom; invert to release and invert again to place on platter, so glaze side is up.

12 TO 16 SERVINGS

CAKE

3 cups all-purpose flour

1 teaspoon baking soda

¾ teaspoon coarse salt

2 tablespoons (packed) minced cinnamon basil or sweet basil leaves

1 ¼ cups vegetable oil, preferably canola oil

1 ¾ cups granulated sugar

3 eggs

2 teaspoons vanilla extract

3 ½ cups unpeeled, coarsely chopped cooking apples, such as Granny Smiths

GLAZE

3 tablespoons unsalted butter

3 tablespoons packed light brown sugar

3 tablespoons granulated sugar

3 tablespoons heavy cream

1 teaspoon vanilla extract

Cinnamon Rhubarb Cake with Cinnamon Basil Custard Sauce

This cake is quite good on its own, but even better dressed up with the custard sauce. It's very moist; be sure it has baked through before removing it from the oven.

CAKE

1½ cups plus 2 tablespoons all-purpose flour, divided

¾ teaspoon baking soda

½ teaspoon coarse salt

½ teaspoon ground cinnamon

1 tablespoon minced cinnamon basil leaves

6 tablespoons unsalted butter, softened

1 cup granulated sugar

1 egg

½ cup nonfat or low-fat buttermilk

½ teaspoon vanilla extract

1¼ cups diced rhubarb

SAUCE

2 cups milk

2-inch cinnamon stick (optional)

(Continued)

1. Preheat oven to 350 degrees. Grease and flour a 9-inch cake pan, or brush pan with Baker's Coating (page 38).

2. In a medium bowl, whisk together 1½ cups flour, baking soda, salt, cinnamon, and cinnamon basil leaves. In another medium bowl, beat butter and sugar on high speed until light and fluffy. Beat in egg.

3. On low speed, beat in flour mixture and buttermilk alternately, beginning and ending with flour mixture and beating just until incorporated. Beat in vanilla. Toss rhubarb with remaining 2 tablespoons flour and fold into batter.

4. Pour into prepared pan and bake 45 to 55 minutes, until cake springs back when lightly pressed. Cool in pan on a wire rack 10 minutes, then turn out onto rack and cool completely.

5. Make sauce: In a medium saucepan, heat milk and cinnamon stick to just below a simmer. In a small bowl, whisk together cinnamon basil leaves, sugar, and eggs just until blended. When milk is hot, very slowly whisk it into the eggs. Return mixture to the saucepan. Cook over medium-low heat, whisking constantly,

until mixture thickens enough to coat the back of a spoon, about 6 minutes. Do not let the sauce boil. Remove from heat and whisk in vanilla. Pour sauce through a strainer into a small bowl. If not using immediately, place a piece of plastic wrap directly on the surface of the sauce and chill.

6. To serve, pour a small amount of sauce onto each plate; top with a slice of cake and drizzle with a little more sauce; garnish with whole leaves.

8 SERVINGS

1 tablespoon minced cinnamon basil leaves

¼ cup granulated sugar

2 eggs

1 teaspoon vanilla extract

GARNISH

Cinnamon basil leaves

Pineapple–Pineapple Mint Upside-Down Cake

If you don't have a cast-iron skillet, here's a good excuse to buy one; I use mine quite often.

Failing that, make the topping in a regular skillet and, as soon as it's cooked, pour it into a 9-

or 10-inch lightly greased cake pan. Expect the baking time to be longer; the cake is done

when the top springs back when pressed lightly with a finger. Also, if you prefer to use

pineapple sage instead of mint, leave it out of the cake and simply use it fresh in the garnish,

after the cake has cooled—its flavor doesn't come through if cooked.

TOPPING

4 tablespoons unsalted
butter

⅔ cup firmly packed
light brown sugar

CAKE

1¾ cups all-purpose
flour

2 teaspoons baking
powder

½ teaspoon coarse salt

2 tablespoon minced
pineapple mint
leaves

2 teaspoons vanilla
extract

1 cup sour cream

1. Preheat oven to 350 degrees.

2. Make topping: In a 9- or 10-inch cast-iron skillet over medium heat, melt butter. Stir in brown sugar and cook, stirring, 4 minutes until bubbly and light brown. Remove from heat, spread caramel to cover bottom of skillet as needed, and let cool.

3. Make cake: In a medium bowl, whisk together flour, baking powder, salt, and pineapple mint leaves. In a small bowl, whisk together vanilla and sour cream. Set both bowls aside. In a large bowl, beat butter and sugar on high speed until light and fluffy, 4 to 8 minutes; don't rush this. Scrape down sides. Beat in eggs 1 at a time, beating well after each addition. With a rubber spatula, fold in half of flour mixture, then sour cream mixture, then remaining flour, mixing just until blended.

4. Set pineapple rings over caramel topping in a single layer

(about 7 rings). Cover with batter, spreading to smooth it. Bake 45 to 50 minutes, until cake is golden and top springs back when pressed lightly with a finger. Remove from oven and run a knife around inside edge of skillet. Top skillet with serving plate and invert cake onto plate.

5. To serve, place a whole pineapple mint leaf in the hole of each pineapple ring. Garnish with additional leaves and serve slices with whipped cream or ice cream if desired.

8 SERVINGS

½ cup (1 stick) unsalted butter, softened

1 cup granulated sugar

3 eggs

1 ripe pineapple, peeled, cored, and cut into ½-inch rings (or use canned rings—about 7)

GARNISH

Pineapple mint leaves; Lightly Sweetened Whipped Cream (recipe follows), or ice cream (optional)

Lightly Sweetened Whipped Cream

1. If you have time, chill a medium bowl and beaters (or whisk, if you're doing this by hand) in the freezer for 20 minutes. Using a hand or stand mixer, beat the cream on low speed for about 10 seconds. Gradually increase to high speed, stopping once to scrape down sides with a spatula. Beat in confectioners' sugar just as cream begins to stiffen. Beat a total of about 55 seconds for soft peaks and 70 seconds for stiff peaks.

1 cup heavy cream

2 tablespoons confectioners' sugar

2. If not using immediately, transfer to a strainer set over a bowl; cover and chill (excess liquid will drain off—if it gets too thick, whisk in a little more cream).

ABOUT 4 TO 6 SERVINGS

Orange Mint Polenta Cake with Orange Compote

I first tried a polenta cake at the cafe at Chez Panisse in Berkeley, California, and immediately fell in love. The cornmeal gives the cake crunch and a buttery, slightly nutty flavor that I strongly prefer to standard cakes, which have never thrilled me. This cake is already moist, but the compote adds even more moisture and dresses up the cake.

CAKE

1 cup yellow cornmeal

¾ cup bleached all-purpose flour

1½ teaspoons baking powder

½ teaspoon coarse salt

1 tablespoon minced orange mint leaves

½ cup (1 stick) unsalted butter, softened

1 cup granulated sugar

2 eggs

2 egg yolks

½ cup orange juice

COMPOTE

6 medium juice oranges

2 tablespoons minced orange mint leaves

2 tablespoons granulated sugar

(Continued)

1. Preheat oven to 350 degrees. Grease and flour a 9-inch cake pan, or brush pan with Baker's Coating (page 38).

2. Make cake: In a medium bowl, whisk together cornmeal, flour, baking powder, salt, and mint leaves. In a large bowl, beat butter and sugar on high speed until light and fluffy. Beat in eggs, then egg yolks, 1 at a time, beating well after each addition. With the mixer on low speed, beat in half the flour mixture just until incorporated. Beat in orange juice, then remaining flour, beating just until blended.

3. Pour batter into prepared cake pan. Bake 35 to 40 minutes, until a tester inserted in the center comes out clean or with just a few crumbs clinging to it. Cool 10 minutes in pan, then turn cake out onto a wire rack to cool completely.

4. Prepare compote 30 minutes to 1 hour before serving: With a sharp knife, cut a small slice off the top and bottom of each orange. Remove peel by slicing from the top to bottom, removing all the white pith. Working over a bowl to catch juice, slice

between membranes to release each orange section. Stir in mint leaves, sugar, and liqueur; let stand to macerate until ready to serve.

5. To serve, dust cake with confectioners' sugar and spoon a few orange slices with a little juice around the top edge. Garnish with mint leaves.

8 SERVINGS

2 tablespoons orange liqueur, such as Grand Marnier (optional)

GARNISH

Confectioners' sugar, orange mint leaves

Lemon Thyme–Buttermilk Cake with Strawberries

I'm not a big fan of cakes, but I do like a simple, fresh cake like this one, especially without a lot of sticky confectioners' sugar frosting. It's perfect on a hot summer day. If you have access to a soft, bleached Southern flour, such as White Lily, you can use it in place of the cake flour.

2 cups cake flour

2 tablespoons minced lemon thyme leaves

Pinch of coarse salt

¾ teaspoon baking soda

½ cup (1 stick) unsalted butter, softened

1¼ cups granulated sugar

3 eggs

2 tablespoons fresh lemon juice

1 cup nonfat or low-fat buttermilk

FILLING AND FROSTING

1 to 1½ pounds strawberries, rinsed

2½ cups heavy cream

¼ cup confectioners' sugar

1. Preheat oven to 350 degrees. Grease and flour two 9-inch cake pans, or brush pans with Baker's Coating (page 38).

2. Whisk together flour, lemon thyme leaves, salt, and baking soda. In a large bowl, beat butter and sugar on high speed until light and fluffy, scraping down sides at least once. Add eggs 1 at a time, beating well after each addition. Beat in lemon juice.

3. Alternately fold in flour mixture and buttermilk with a rubber spatula, beginning and ending with flour, mixing until just combined. Divide batter between prepared pans, spreading it more thickly around the edges.

4. Bake cakes 30 to 35 minutes, until tops are golden and cake springs back when lightly pressed with a finger. Cool in pans on a rack 10 minutes; turn cakes out onto racks and let cool completely.

5. Make filling and frosting: Stem and thinly slice enough of the strawberries to measure 1½ cups. Mash them with a fork or pastry blender until coarsely mashed. In a large bowl, whip the cream on high speed; just when soft peaks form, beat in confectioners' sugar and continue beating until stiff peaks form.

6. Fold mashed berries into 1 cup of the whipped cream. Place 1 cake layer on serving platter (trim the cakes if necessary to obtain flat tops). Pipe or spoon a ½-inch rim of plain whipped cream around the outer edge to act as a dam for the filling. Spoon the strawberry whipped cream into the center and spread it to the edge of the plain whipped cream. Cover with remaining cake layer and frost all over with remaining plain whipped cream, swirling it or piping it decoratively onto the top. Slice remaining strawberries in half and use them to garnish the cake, standing them upside down around the base, anchored gently in the cream.

12 SERVINGS

Blueberry-Mint Layer Cake

Light, fresh and gorgeous—this is my kind of layer cake. If you can't get fresh berries, use well-thawed frozen ones. After I've spread on a smooth layer of whipped cream frosting, I pipe out a rim of rosettes around the base and top of the cake, garnishing with a few berries and mint leaves. If you don't have a pastry bag and tips, simply pile the berries in the center of the cake and arrange a few around the rim.

2 cups all-purpose flour

¾ teaspoon coarse salt

1½ teaspoons baking powder

½ cup nonfat or low-fat buttermilk

2 teaspoons vanilla extract

3 eggs

1¼ cups granulated sugar

¾ cup heavy cream

FILLING AND FROSTING

1 pint blueberries, rinsed and picked over, divided

⅓ cup granulated sugar

2 tablespoons fresh lemon juice

2 tablespoons minced mint leaves

4 teaspoons cornstarch

(Continued)

1. Preheat oven to 350 degrees. Grease and flour two 9-inch round cake pans, or brush pans with Baker's Coating (page 38).

2. In a medium bowl, whisk together flour, salt, and baking powder; set aside. In a small bowl, whisk together buttermilk and vanilla; set aside. In a large bowl, beat eggs with sugar on high speed until thick; batter should fall in a ribbon when beaters are lifted. With mixer on low speed or by hand, alternately mix in flour and buttermilk mixtures, beginning and ending with flour. Mix just until combined.

3. In another bowl, with clean beaters, beat cream until stiff peaks form; gently fold into batter. Pour batter into prepared pans and smooth the tops. Bake for 30 to 35 minutes, until a tester inserted in the middle comes out clean. Cool 10 minutes on a rack, then turn cakes out onto rack to cool completely.

4. While cakes are baking, prepare filling: In a small saucepan, combine 1½ cups blueberries, granulated sugar, lemon juice, and mint leaves. Cook over medium heat, stirring, until sugar dissolves. Stir together cornstarch and water until no lumps

remain and add to blueberries; bring to a boil, and stir and cook about 1 minute, until mixture is thick and clear. Set aside to cool completely, stirring occasionally.

5. To finish cake: In a large bowl, whip the cream on high speed; just when soft peaks form, beat in confectioners' sugar, and continue beating until stiff peaks form. Place 1 cake layer on a serving platter (trim the cakes if necessary to obtain flat tops). Pipe or spoon a ½-inch rim of whipped cream around the outer edge to act as a dam for the filling. Spoon the blueberry filling into the center and spread it to the edge of the whipped cream. Cover with remaining cake layer and frost all over with remaining whipped cream, swirling it or piping it decoratively onto the top. Arrange some or all of the remaining blueberries on top and garnish with mint leaves around the base.

12 SERVINGS

¼ cup water

2¼ cups heavy cream

5 tablespoons confectioners' sugar

GARNISH

Mint leaves

Basil-Balsamic Strawberry Shortcakes

During the local strawberry season, my mother would periodically throw dietary cautions to the wind and serve us strawberry shortcakes for dinner, complete with whipped cream. I never thought I'd change that tradition, but the basil isn't too radical a change, and she approves. Use a good-quality balsamic; just a few drops greatly enhance the flavor of the berries.

FILLING

1 ½ pounds strawberries, rinsed and stemmed

1 ½ teaspoons balsamic vinegar

2 tablespoons granulated sugar

2 tablespoons minced basil leaves

SHORTCAKES

3 cups bleached all-purpose flour

4 teaspoons baking powder

¾ teaspoon coarse salt

¼ cup granulated sugar

1 ¾ cups heavy cream, or more as needed

GARNISH

Confectioners' sugar;

Lightly Sweetened Whipped Cream (page 43)

1. Preheat oven to 425 degrees.

2. Make filling: Slice the strawberries into a medium bowl. Sprinkle with the balsamic vinegar and stir well. Stir in sugar and basil leaves; cover with plastic and set aside to macerate.

3. Make shortcakes: Whisk together flour, baking powder, salt, and sugar. Stir in cream with a spatula or fork, adding more cream 1 tablespoon at a time if needed to make a soft dough. Turn onto a lightly floured board and press dough into a rough disk. Roll out to ¾-inch thickness and cut into 3-inch rounds. Press any scraps together and re-roll; you need at least 6 shortcakes but may get more. Place on a parchment paper–lined baking sheet and bake 15 minutes, until lightly browned. Let cool 5 to 10 minutes before serving.

3. To serve, split each shortcake in half. Divide the berries among the cake bottoms, drizzling them with liquid from the bottom of the bowl (the basil will have migrated there). Replace shortcake tops, dust them with confectioners' sugar, and garnish with dollops of whipped cream.

6 SERVINGS

Lemon Thyme–Raspberry Pudding Cakes

Easy and delicate, pudding cakes make their own sauce in the bottom of the ramekin. If you don't have ramekins, use a 9-inch-square dish. The tea towel in the pan keeps the ramekins from sliding.

1. Butter six 6-ounce ramekins (measuring about 3 inches across) and sprinkle lightly with sugar. Put 8 raspberries in the bottom of each ramekin; set aside in a shallow baking pan lined with a tea towel. Preheat oven to 350 degrees.

2. In a medium bowl, beat egg yolks, milk, butter, ¼ cup lemon juice, and lemon thyme leaves on medium speed until well blended. Beat in ¾ cup sugar and flour until well blended. In another bowl with clean beaters, beat egg whites until they are stiff. Fold a quarter of the whites into yolk mixture to lighten it, then gently fold in remaining whites. Divide batter among ramekins.

3. Fill a pitcher with hot tap water. Place baking pan in oven and quickly pour in enough hot water to come halfway up the sides of the ramekins. Bake 30 minutes, until just set.

4. Meanwhile, puree remaining raspberries in a food processor with 2 tablespoons sugar and 2 tablespoons lemon juice. Press through a sieve to remove seeds; taste, adjusting sugar and lemon juice as needed.

5. To serve, set warm ramekins on dessert plates and drizzle tops of cakes with raspberry sauce; garnish plates with lemon thyme sprigs.

12 ounces raspberries (if frozen, thaw and drain)

3 egg yolks

1 ¼ cups milk

2 tablespoons unsalted butter, melted and cooled

¼ cup plus 2 tablespoons fresh lemon juice, divided

1 tablespoon minced lemon thyme leaves

¾ cup plus 2 tablespoons granulated sugar, divided

¼ cup all-purpose flour

3 egg whites

GARNISH

Lemon thyme sprigs

6 SERVINGS

Cheesecake with Tarragon Cherries

Rich and smooth, this easy cheesecake has a topping with a twist. Don't worry if the top cracks; you'll cover that with the cherries. If you don't have chocolate wafers on hand, try the plain crust variation—I can't decide which I like better! Don't use nonfat cream cheese, although neufchatel would be OK.

CRUST

1 ¼ cups chocolate wafer crumbs (about half of a 9-ounce package)

3 tablespoons unsalted butter, melted

2 tablespoons granulated sugar

FILLING

1 pound cream cheese, softened

½ cup granulated sugar

2 eggs

2 cups sour cream

2 teaspoons vanilla extract

TOPPING

1 16-ounce bag frozen sweet cherries

2 teaspoons minced tarragon leaves

(Continued)

1. Preheat oven to 350 degrees.

2. Mix crumbs, butter, and sugar for crust and press into the bottom of a greased 9-inch springform pan (wrap outside of pan with foil if you're worried about its seal). Bake 10 minutes.

3. Meanwhile, make filling: In a large bowl, beat cream cheese on low speed until smooth and fluffy. Beat in sugar. Beat in eggs 1 at a time, then beat in sour cream and vanilla just until blended. Pour over hot crust and bake 45 minutes; when done, cheesecake will feel dry on the top and be barely jiggly in the middle. Remove from oven and let cool on a wire rack, then chill at least 4 hours.

4. Make topping: Put cherries, tarragon, lemon juice, sugar, and ⅓ cup water into a small saucepan. Stir and cook over medium-high heat until mixture comes to a boil. In a small bowl, stir together cornstarch and remaining ⅓ cup water. Pour into cherry mixture and bring to a boil, stirring constantly and scraping the bottom of the pan. Cook about 30 seconds until mixture thickens and is no longer cloudy. Cool, stirring often, then cover and chill.

5. To serve, use a knife dipped in hot water to slice the cheesecake.

Top each slice with some of the cherries, or spread the cherries over the top of the whole cheesecake before slicing.

16 SERVINGS

VARIATION: For a plain crust, use ⅓ cup light brown sugar (packed), 1 cup all-purpose flour, and ⅓ cup butter, melted. Stir these together with a spatula or fork until well-blended, and press evenly into a greased 9-inch springform pan. Bake in the pre-heated 350-degree oven for 15 minutes; continue following directions at step 2.

1 tablespoon fresh
   lemon juice

½ cup granulated sugar

⅔ cup water, divided

2 tablespoons
   cornstarch

Petite Lime Balm Cheesecakes

This easy recipe was inspired by a Key lime pie–flavored ice cream I ate in Blowing Rock, North Carolina, which includes chocolate cookie pieces—a great combination, and a nice change from a standard cheesecake crust. My supermarket stocks the cookies with its ice cream cones and toppings.

12 thin chocolate wafer cookies

8 ounces cream cheese, softened

¾ cup granulated sugar

2 eggs

2 tablespoons fresh lime juice

⅓ cup minced lime balm leaves

GARNISH

Lightly Sweetened Whipped Cream (page 43) whipped until stiff peaks form; 2 teaspoons minced lime balm leaves

1. Preheat oven to 350 degrees. Put paper liners into 12 standard muffin cups; press 1 cookie into each (you may have to press down a bit to get it flat on the bottom).

2. In a medium bowl, beat cream cheese on low speed until light and fluffy. Scrape down sides and beat in sugar. Scrape down sides again and beat in eggs 1 at a time, blending well. Beat in lime juice, then ⅓ cup lime balm leaves until blended. Divide batter among muffin cups. Bake 20 minutes until puffed. Cool on a wire rack (cheesecakes may fall), then chill in refrigerator, covered.

3. To serve: Pipe or spoon whipped cream onto cheesecakes; sprinkle with lime balm leaves.

1 DOZEN CHEESECAKES

Pies,

Tarts,

and Tortes

Rhubarb-Pecan Pie

Every herb book I've read says to use angelica with rhubarb to reduce the amount of sugar needed with a tart pie filling. I don't know why, but it works.

1. Preheat oven to 400 degrees.

2. On a lightly floured surface, roll out 1 pie dough disk to about an 11-inch circle, lifting and turning the dough to keep it from sticking to the surface. Fold the dough in quarters and transfer it to a 9-inch pie pan, preferably glass. Unfold and gently tuck it into the sides of the pan.

3. Whisk together sugar, angelica leaves, cornstarch, orange zest, salt, and pecans. Stir in rhubarb. Pile into pie crust, mounding slightly in the center. Using a vegetable peeler, peel thin slices of butter and distribute them over top of pie filling.

4. Roll out remaining dough as above. Cut into 10 equal strips, each about ½-inch wide. Lay 5 strips over filling, evenly spaced. Weave remaining 5 strips across the first 5, creating a lattice crust, and pinch and flute the ends to seal them to the bottom crust. Brush strips and rim lightly with beaten egg and sprinkle with turbinado sugar.

5. Place the pie plate on a rimmed baking sheet and bake 40 minutes. Reduce heat to 350 degrees and bake 25 to 35 minutes more, until crust is golden and filling is thick and bubbly, covering edges with foil if they brown too quickly. Cool on a wire rack.

6. Serve pie warm or at room temperature with ice cream or whipped cream if desired.

1 recipe chilled Pie Dough (page 76), split into 2 disks

1 cup granulated sugar

3 tablespoons minced angelica leaves

¼ cup cornstarch

1 tablespoon grated orange zest

½ cup chopped pecans

Pinch of coarse salt

5 cups rhubarb (about 2 pounds), diced

1 tablespoon unsalted butter

1 egg, lightly beaten

1 tablespoon turbinado sugar

GARNISH

Vanilla ice cream or Lightly Sweetened Whipped Cream (page 43), optional

8 SERVINGS

Blueberry-Basil Pie

Although I prefer pies made with fresh berries, the season always seems too short. Since I can grow or buy basil year-round, I wanted to develop a pie that would work equally well (if not better) with frozen berries. To make this with fresh berries, use 6 cups berries but only 3 tablespoons tapioca.

6 cups (3 1-pound bags) frozen blueberries

1 recipe chilled Pie Dough (page 76), split into 2 disks

1 cup granulated sugar

½ cup whole basil leaves

¼ cup instant tapioca

1 tablespoon fresh lemon juice

1 to 2 teaspoons heavy cream

1 tablespoon turbinado sugar or granulated sugar

1. Using 1 or 2 paper towel–lined baking sheets, turn berries out in a single layer to thaw somewhat for at least 30 minutes. (I like a juicy pie with berries that stay plump; if you want a firmer pie, let berries thaw almost completely, at least 1 hour, and be sure they are drained well.)

2. Preheat oven to 450 degrees. On a lightly floured surface, roll out 1 disk of pie dough to about an 11-inch circle, lifting and turning the dough to keep it from sticking to the surface. Fold the dough in quarters and transfer it to a 9-inch pie pan, preferably glass. Unfold and gently tuck it into the sides of the pan.

3. Place granulated sugar and basil leaves in a food processor; process until basil is minced into the sugar. Turn into a large bowl and stir in tapioca.

4. With your hands, transfer berries to the bowl with the sugar, letting any large ice crystals drop onto the paper towels. Sprinkle the berries with the lemon juice, then toss berries and sugar together gently with a spatula. Turn berry mixture into the pie crust, mounding berries in the center.

5. Roll out the remaining disk of dough as above and place over the berries. Tuck under the overhang of both pieces of dough and crimp the edges; cut a small steam vent into center. Brush dough gently with cream and sprinkle with turbinado sugar.

6. Place pie on a baking sheet to catch any drips; bake for 10 minutes. Lower the heat to 400 degrees and bake 35 to 40 minutes more, until the top is a deep golden color. Remove from the oven and let cool on a rack before cutting.

8 SERVINGS

Cantaloupe Cloud Pie

This is a wonderful surprise; how often do you eat cantaloupe in a pie? Cantaloupes vary in their sweetness; make sure to use a very ripe one, but you may still need more sugar, which you can add when whipping the cream. The pie is great on its own, but try the blueberry topping for a terrific taste and texture contrast.

CRUST

1 ¼ cups graham cracker crumbs

¼ cup granulated sugar

5 tablespoons unsalted butter, melted

FILLING

2 tablespoons (packed) whole lime basil leaves

⅓ cup granulated sugar

1 envelope plain powdered gelatin

1 small, very ripe cantaloupe, halved and seeded

¼ cup fresh lime juice (or use bottled Key lime juice)

1 cup heavy cream

2 to 4 tablespoons confectioners' sugar, as needed

(Continued)

1. Preheat oven to 350 degrees and lightly grease a 9-inch pie plate.

2. Make crust: In a small bowl, stir together cracker crumbs, sugar, and butter until blended. Press evenly into bottom and sides of pie plate. Bake 10 to 15 minutes until lightly browned; cool completely on a wire rack.

3. Make filling: Grind lime basil leaves with sugar in a food processor or blender until finely ground. Transfer to a small saucepan and whisk in gelatin. Remove flesh from cantaloupe and puree in processor or blender. Measure out 2 cups of the puree and pour into saucepan; let mixture stand without stirring for 1 minute.

4. Place saucepan over low heat and whisk for 4 minutes, until gelatin is dissolved. Remove from heat and whisk in lime juice. Pour into a small bowl and chill until cold but not set. Taste; if it isn't sweet enough, use the confectioners' sugar as needed when whipping cream.

5. In a medium bowl, whip cream until stiff peaks form; if using sugar, add it when cream just begins to stiffen. Fold cream into

cantaloupe mixture gently but thoroughly; pour into graham cracker crust. Cover and chill until set (it will be a slightly soft set).

6. Serve as is, or make topping: Arrange blueberries over top of pie; melt jelly with water over low heat and brush over berries to glaze them.

8 SERVINGS

TOPPING (OPTIONAL)

1 pint blueberries

1 tablespoon apple or
  red currant jelly

2 teaspoons water

Apple-Sage Tarte Tatin

Granny Smiths are classic cooking apples and work well here; I use Arkansas Black when I can find them.

6 apples, peeled, cored, each sliced into 8 wedges

1 tablespoon fresh lemon juice

¾ cup firmly packed light brown sugar

6 tablespoons unsalted butter

¾ cup granulated sugar

3 tablespoons minced sage leaves

½ recipe chilled Pie Dough (page 76)

GARNISH

Fresh sage leaves; Lightly Sweetened Whipped Cream (page 43), optional

1. Preheat oven to 425 degrees.

2. Put apples, lemon juice, and brown sugar in a large bowl and toss to mix; set aside. Melt butter in a 9- or 10-inch cast-iron skillet (or other heavy, oven-safe skillet), and stir in granulated sugar. Cook over medium-high heat, stirring, until mixture turns pale golden. Add apple mixture and cook, tossing occasionally to coat apples, for 5 minutes. Add sage leaves and cook 5 minutes more, stirring occasionally. Set aside while you roll out the dough.

3. On a lightly floured surface, roll out the dough to about a 10-inch circle for a 9-inch skillet, or an 11-inch circle for a 10-inch skillet, lifting dough and turning to prevent sticking to the surface. Fold the dough in half or quarters and place it over the apples in the skillet. Unfold the dough, tuck the overhang under the edge of the dough into the skillet, and cut 4 slits in a circle at the center of the dough. Bake 20 minutes until the crust is deep golden.

4. Using heavy oven mitts, remove skillet from oven and shake lightly to dislodge any stuck apples. Place a serving platter over the pan and, gripping the pan and plate lightly together, flip the tart over onto the platter. Let stand a few minutes before serving, or serve at room temperature. Do not refrigerate. Garnish with a few fresh sage leaves, and serve plain or with whipped cream.

8 SERVINGS

Tarragon Pear Galette

This flat, open-faced pie has an appealingly rustic look as it requires no pie or tart pans, and the filling is simple and rustic as well. It is best if eaten the day it's made, to keep it from getting soggy.

1. Preheat oven to 400 degrees.

2. On a lightly floured surface, roll out pie dough to a 12-inch circle. Transfer to a parchment paper–lined, rimmed baking sheet (easiest to do if you fold dough in half or quarters first). Fold in a 1-inch rim around the dough circle. Brush the rim lightly with beaten egg, then flute the edge or imprint it with the tines of a fork. Sprinkle with 3 tablespoons turbinado sugar.

3. Top with pears, arranging slices in concentric circles. Stir together butter and tarragon leaves. Brush pears with about 2 tablespoons of the butter mixture. Sprinkle with remaining turbinado sugar.

4. Bake galette 20 minutes; reduce heat to 350 degrees and bake 20 to 25 minutes more, until pears are tender and pastry is crisp. Remove from oven and brush pears with remaining butter mixture.

5. Serve galette warm or at room temperature, with ice cream or whipped cream if desired.

8 SERVINGS

½ recipe Pie Dough (page 76)

1 egg, lightly beaten

6 tablespoons turbinado or granulated sugar, divided

3 firm-ripe pears, preferably Bosc or D'Anjou, peeled, cored, and thinly sliced

3 tablespoons unsalted butter, melted

1½ tablespoons minced tarragon leaves

GARNISH

Vanilla ice cream or Lightly Sweetened Whipped Cream (page 43), optional

Raspberry-Lime Tart

The filling for this tart is based on a low-fat lemon curd recipe by cookbook author Susan Purdy, which I love for its light texture and less-cloying flavor than standard curd recipes. The filling, like that for the Lemon-Lime Phyllo Tartlets on page 68, can also be used in other tart shells, in a parfait with berries and whipped cream, or as a filling or topping for a simple sponge cake.

¼ cup (packed) whole lime balm leaves

¾ cup granulated sugar

2 tablespoons cornstarch

¼ teaspoon coarse salt

¾ cup hot water

½ cup fresh lime juice (or use bottled Key lime juice)

½ cup heavy cream

1 baked and cooled Tart Crust (page 77)

½ pint raspberries

GARNISH

Lime balm leaves; vanilla ice cream or Lightly Sweetened Whipped Cream (page 43), optional

1. In a food processor or blender, whiz together lime balm leaves and sugar until leaves are finely ground. Transfer to a small saucepan and whisk in cornstarch and salt. Whisk in water and lime juice. Place over medium heat and bring to a boil, whisking constantly; boil 1 minute, until mixture is clear and thickened (it will thicken much more upon chilling). Remove from heat and whisk in cream.

2. Pour filling into crust, spreading evenly. Chill until cold and set.

3. Arrange raspberries over filling and garnish with a few lime balm leaves. Serve plain or with a scoop of vanilla ice cream or whipped cream.

8 SERVINGS

Apple-Thyme Tarts

I developed this recipe two years before I started work on this book; it was one of the early successes that got me excited about working with herbs in my baking. Thyme is a delicate flavor that blends nicely with the apples and the buttery (and easy) pastry.

1. Preheat oven to 400 degrees. Slice apples into ¼-inch slices.

2. In a large skillet over medium-high heat, melt butter; add apples and cook 5 minutes. Stir in thyme and sugar and sauté until apples begin to soften, about 3 minutes. Add lemon juice and cook 30 seconds more. Remove from heat and set aside.

3. On a lightly floured surface, roll out 1 pastry sheet into a 13-by-9-inch rectangle and, using a small plate as a guide, cut out two 6-inch circles from opposite corners of the sheet. Place on a lightly greased or parchment-lined baking sheet. Make raised rims for these circles by using plate and remaining pastry to cut out four ¼-inch-wide crescents. Brush egg around edge of pastry circles and top with crescents to create rim; brush these with egg. Repeat with second sheet of pastry, using a second baking sheet.

4. Distribute apples over pastry circles, leaving the rims bare. Bake 25 to 30 minutes, reversing sheets after 15 minutes from top to bottom and front to back, until pastry is cooked through and crisp. Serve warm, either plain or with a scoop of ice cream or whipped cream.

4 SERVINGS

4 medium Granny Smith apples (about 1 ½ pounds), peeled and cored

3 tablespoons unsalted butter

1 tablespoon (packed) whole thyme leaves

¼ cup granulated sugar

1 ½ teaspoons fresh lemon juice

2 sheets frozen puff pastry (1 17¼-ounce package), thawed

1 egg, lightly beaten

GARNISH

Vanilla ice cream or Lightly Sweetened Whipped Cream (page 43), optional

Starfruit-Mint Tartlets

The tartlet shells, which take a bit of time to bake, can be made a day or two ahead and stored in an airtight container. The recipe can be cut in half (note that half of ⅓ cup sugar is 3 tablespoons), but I never want to make just four! You can substitute regular mint, if you prefer, and if you can't find starfruit, try using kiwi instead (you'll need about 4, peeled and thinly sliced).

SHELLS

1 tablespoon minced orange mint leaves

1½ cups bleached all-purpose flour

⅓ cup granulated sugar

½ cup (1 stick) cold unsalted butter, cut into 16 pieces

FILLING

8 ounces cream cheese, cold

½ cup confectioners' sugar

2 tablespoons minced orange mint leaves

½ cup heavy cream

2 teaspoons fresh lemon juice

3 starfruit, thinly sliced, seeds removed

2 tablespoons apple jelly

GARNISH

Orange mint leaves

1. Preheat oven to 350 degrees.

2. Make shells: Whisk mint leaves, flour, and sugar together. Cut in butter with your fingertips until mixture resembles coarse crumbs, then knead dough until it just forms a ball. Divide among eight 4-inch tartlet pans, preferably with removable bottoms, and press evenly onto bottom and sides. Prick bottoms all over with a fork. Bake 30 minutes, until golden brown. Cool on a wire rack.

3. Make filling: With a hand or stand mixer, beat cream cheese, confectioners' sugar, and mint leaves until smooth. Beat in cream until mixture thickens slightly; beat in lemon juice. Divide among shells.

4. Arrange starfruit slices decoratively over filling. In a small saucepan over low heat, heat jelly until it liquefies. Brush gently over fruit to glaze; garnish with mint leaves. Serve immediately, gently dislodging tartlets from tins (bottoms should slide off), or chill up to 1 day ahead.

8 SERVINGS

Anise Sugar Tartlets

I have an old clipping in my recipe files that seems to be about Canadian sugar pies made just with sugar, cream, and eggs. I'd never tried the recipe before, but thought it would be good with anise—and it is. Quick to make, they're also very rich. You'll have a lot of leftover puff pastry scraps; you can make small cookies from them by coating them with sugar and cutting them into squares or strips. Bake them on a parchment paper–lined baking sheet at the same time as the tartlets, until golden and crisp, about 20 minutes.

1. Preheat oven to 400 degrees.

2. Unfold puff pastry sheets and cut each in quarters. Press dough into eight 4-inch tartlet tins; remove excess dough by running a rolling pin over the tops of the tins to sever it. Set tins on a baking sheet.

3. In a food processor or blender, grind anise hyssop leaves and ½ cup brown sugar until leaves are minced. Transfer to a medium bowl and whisk in remaining ½ cup brown sugar and cream, flour, and eggs until no lumps remain. Divide among tins.

4. Bake 30 to 35 minutes, until pastry is browned and crisp and filling is puffed and set (it will sink as it cools). Let stand 5 minutes on a rack, then remove from tins. Serve warm; these are good plain but also go well with ice cream or whipped cream.

8 SERVINGS

2 sheets frozen puff pastry (1 17¼-ounce package), thawed

¼ cup (packed) whole anise hyssop leaves

1 cup packed light brown sugar, divided

¾ cup heavy cream

2 teaspoons all-purpose flour

2 eggs

GARNISH

Vanilla ice cream or Lightly Sweetened Whipped Cream (page 43), optional

Lemon-Lime Phyllo Tartlets

This is a pretty dessert with a great texture contrast. I like to see the flecks of the basils in the filling, but you could strain them out when pouring the filling into a bowl if you wish. I prefer to use fresh juices for the filling, but I keep a bottle of Key lime juice on hand, and that works well here. If you can find fresh phyllo, use it, as it will be a bit more pliable than frozen.

FILLING

4 eggs

¾ cup (1 ½ sticks) unsalted butter, diced

1 cup granulated sugar

2 tablespoons minced lemon basil leaves

2 tablespoons minced lime basil leaves

¼ cup fresh lemon juice

¼ cup fresh lime juice

SHELLS

6 sheets phyllo, thawed if frozen

4 tablespoons unsalted butter, melted

About 6 teaspoons granulated sugar, divided

(Continued)

1. Make the filling: In a medium saucepan, whisk together eggs, butter, sugar, both basil leaves, lemon juice, and lime juice. Cook, whisking constantly, over medium-low heat until just thickened; once butter has melted this will take 3 to 5 minutes. Do not let the mixture boil. Pour into a bowl, cover surface directly with plastic wrap, and chill until shells are baked and cooled.

2. Make the shells: Preheat oven to 325 degrees and lightly oil 8 standard-size muffin cups. Place 1 phyllo sheet on a work surface; keep remaining sheets covered with a damp towel. Brush phyllo with melted butter and sprinkle with 1 teaspoon sugar. Cover with 3 more sheets, repeating buttering and sugaring of each layer. Cut into six 5-inch squares, discarding phyllo scraps. Press each square gently into a muffin cup (the tops of the squares will rest on the rims of the cups). Working quickly, place 1 more phyllo sheet on work surface, buttering and sugaring as above, and top with last sheet, buttering and sugaring it. Cut the sheets in half to form two 8-by-12-inch rectangles; put one rectangle on top of the other. Cut this into two 5-inch squares, discarding excess phyllo scraps, and press into cups as above.

3. Bake cups 8 to 10 minutes, until golden and crisp. Let pan cool on a wire rack.

4. To serve, divide filling among the phyllo cups. Garnish with lemon or lime basil leaves and top with a dollop of whipped cream that drapes down the side of the cup, if desired (I prefer them plain, but they won't look as dressed up).

8 SERVINGS

Chocolate Mint Meringue Torte

This is based on my mother's recipe for Bridge Meringue Torte, which she made for my baptism dinner. Since I was only a month old, I can't remember that one, but I've loved all the tortes she's made since. Her version had a plain meringue with pecans; this is significantly different but still has the nice balance of sweet meringue and rich but unsweetened whipped cream. Note that it needs to be made ahead; the chilling time allows the cream to soften the meringue layers slightly.

6 egg whites, at room temperature

1 ½ teaspoons vanilla extract

½ teaspoon cream of tartar

1 ¼ cups granulated sugar

2 tablespoons minced chocolate mint leaves

¼ cup Dutch-process cocoa

2 milk chocolate bars (such as Hershey's) about 1 ½ ounces each

2 cups heavy cream

GARNISH

Whole mint leaves

1. Preheat oven to 275 degrees. Trace 9-inch circles on 2 pieces of parchment paper; flip the papers over and place on 2 baking sheets.

2. In a large bowl, beat egg whites on high until they form soft peaks. Beat in vanilla and cream of tartar. Very gradually beat in sugar until whites form very stiff peaks; quickly beat in mint leaves. Sift cocoa over the whites and quickly beat in (this is a good time to use the towel-over-the-mixer method described on page 11, as cocoa dust will fly everywhere).

3. Divide whites between baking sheets and spread onto the two 9-inch circles. Bake for 1 hour. Turn off the oven, but leave the meringues inside with the door closed for at least 2 hours, until cooled.

4. With a vegetable peeler, shave chocolate bars into slightly curling strips. In a large bowl, beat cream on high until it forms stiff peaks. Fold half the chocolate curls into the cream. Carefully

peel parchment from 1 meringue layer and place on serving platter. Spread with a third of the whipped cream. Top with remaining meringue layer and cover top and sides with remaining cream. Sprinkle with remaining chocolate curls. Cover with plastic wrap and chill 8 hours or overnight (to cover, gently stick toothpicks into the meringue and drape plastic over the picks).

5. To serve, garnish torte with mint leaves and cut into wedges with a sharp knife.

8 SERVINGS

Blueberry Bavarian Torte with Lemon Thyme Sauce

It's probably easy to figure out my dessert preferences from reading this book; I love creamy, cool, light (sometimes deceptively light, as they have lots of cream) desserts. This torte fits that description perfectly. Note that this recipe uses 2 pints of fresh blueberries.

TORTE

1 ½ cups shortbread cookie crumbs

2 tablespoons unsalted butter, melted

1 envelope unflavored gelatin

½ cup water, divided

1 pint blueberries, washed and picked over

¾ cup granulated sugar

1 tablespoon fresh lemon juice

2 cups heavy cream

SAUCE

1 tablespoon cornstarch

½ cup water, divided

1 pint blueberries, washed and picked over

½ cup granulated sugar

1 tablespoon minced lemon thyme leaves

2 tablespoons fresh lemon juice

1. Preheat oven to 350 degrees.

2. In a small bowl, stir together shortbread crumbs and butter. Press evenly into the bottom of a 9-inch springform pan. Bake for 10 minutes; cool completely on a wire rack.

3. In a small bowl, sprinkle gelatin over ¼ cup water and set aside. Puree 1 pint blueberries in a food processor or blender. Transfer to a medium saucepan and stir in remaining ¼ cup water and the sugar. Bring to a simmer over medium heat, stirring to dissolve sugar. Remove from heat; stir in lemon juice and softened gelatin until gelatin is dissolved. Cool to room temperature.

4. In a large bowl, whip cream until stiff peaks form. Fold in cooled blueberry mixture gently but thoroughly. Pour over cooled crust and smooth top. Cover and chill 4 to 24 hours.

5. Make sauce: In a small bowl, stir together cornstarch and ¼ cup water; set aside. In a small saucepan, stir together blueberries, sugar, ¼ cup water, and lemon thyme leaves. Bring to a simmer over medium heat, stirring to dissolve sugar. Add cornstarch

mixture and cook, stirring, 1 minute, until sauce is clear and slightly thickened. Remove from heat and stir in lemon juice. Chill until ready to serve torte.

6. To serve, run a thin knife around the inside edge of the springform pan to loosen the torte. Remove sides from pan and place torte on a serving platter. Slice with a thin knife, wiping it clean between slices. Serve with a little sauce poured over the top and more sauce on the side.

12 TO 16 SERVINGS

Lavender Plum Kuchen

My mother's famed plum kuchen is easy to make and works well for both dessert and breakfast; I've spiced it up a bit with lavender instead of cinnamon—the lavender balances the slightly tart plums.

1¼ cups bleached all-purpose flour

½ cup granulated sugar, divided

Pinch of coarse salt

½ cup (1 stick) cold unsalted butter, cut into 16 pieces

2 egg yolks

1 tablespoon water

5 or 6 ripe red plums (about 1 pound), unpeeled, thinly sliced

1½ teaspoons dried lavender flowers, or 2 teaspoons fresh

GARNISH

Lightly Sweetened Whipped Cream (page 43), optional

1. Preheat oven to 350 degrees; butter a 9-inch tart pan set on a rimmed baking sheet.

2. Whisk together flour, ¼ cup sugar, and salt in a medium bowl, or process briefly in a food processor. Cut in butter by hand or by pulsing in processor until coarse crumbs form. Whisk together egg yolks and water and stir into flour mixture; knead gently or pulse in processor until dough just forms a ball.

3. Press dough into prepared pan. Place plum slices, slightly overlapping, in concentric circles over dough. Stir together remaining ¼ cup sugar and the lavender and sprinkle evenly over plums.

3. Bake 45 minutes, until plums are tender and pastry is golden; cool on a wire rack at least 15 minutes before serving. Serve warm or at room temperature, plain or with a dollop of whipped cream.

8 SERVINGS

Mixed Berry Turnovers

I've been making some version of these turnovers since I was a teenager—they make a great, simple dessert and fabulous breakfast leftovers. Eat them while they're warm and fresh out of the oven, before the pastry softens; reheat leftovers in a 350-degree oven until warm and crisp. Frozen berries, thoroughly thawed, may also be used.

1. Preheat oven to 425 degrees.

2. Stir together sugar, tapioca, and lemon balm leaves. Stir in lemon juice and gently fold in berries.

3. On a lightly floured surface, gently roll out 1 puff pastry sheet to a 12-inch square. Cut into 4 squares. Put about ⅓ cup of the berry mixture in the center of each square and dot with a little butter. Brush egg along the bottom and right edges of the pastry squares; fold the dry edges over to form triangles and crimp the edges very well to seal them. Place on a parchment paper–lined baking sheet (or line a baking sheet with a piece of well-greased foil). Repeat with second pastry sheet.

4. Bake turnovers for 20 minutes, or until golden and crisp. Serve warm.

8 SERVINGS

½ cup granulated sugar

3 tablespoons instant tapioca

2 tablespoons minced lemon balm leaves

1 tablespoon fresh lemon juice

4 cups berries, such as blueberries, raspberries, and/or blackberries, rinsed, picked over, and dried

2 sheets frozen puff pastry (1 17¼-ounce package), thawed

2 tablespoons unsalted butter

1 egg, lightly beaten

Pie Dough

This is a somewhat unorthodox method of making pie crusts, and the dough may be softer than you're used to, but it works beautifully and tastes good; it's my standard dough. This recipe doubles easily.

2¾ cups flour, preferably bleached all-purpose

2 teaspoons coarse salt

½ cup (1 stick) cold unsalted butter, cut into 16 pieces

¾ cup vegetable shortening, frozen for 10 minutes

½ cup iced water

1. With a hand-held or stand mixer, combine flour and salt on low speed. Add butter and continue mixing until it resembles coarse crumbs. Gradually add shortening, beating until mixture begins to clump up. Add water (discard any ice chips first) all at once and beat until dough begins to hold together.

2. Gather dough into a ball with your hands, divide into 2 pieces, and flatten each piece into a disk. Wrap each in plastic wrap and chill until ready to use, at least 1 hour and up to 4 days. For longer storage, overwrap the plastic in foil or place disks in a freezer bag and freeze. Thaw overnight in the refrigerator before using.

2 9- TO 11-INCH CRUSTS

Tart Crust

1. Preheat oven to 400 degrees.

2. Whisk together flour, cornstarch, sugar, and salt, or pulse them briefly in a food processor. Cut in butter by hand or pulse in processor until mixture resembles coarse crumbs. Stir in egg yolk or add it to processor; mix until dough begins to clump together.

3. Press dough together by hand until it forms a ball. Press evenly into the bottom and sides of a 9- or 10-inch removable-bottom tart pan. Prick all over with a fork.

4. Bake for 20 minutes, until just golden. Cool completely on a wire rack.

1 9- OR 10-INCH CRUST

1 cup bleached all-purpose flour

¼ cup cornstarch

¼ cup sugar

Pinch of coarse salt

½ cup (1 stick) unsalted butter, cut into 16 pieces

1 egg yolk

Crisps,

Cobblers,

Custards,

and Puddings

Individual Cranberry-Peach Crisps

These are wonderful on a cold winter day (and great for breakfast if there are leftovers). To serve them, try putting the ramekin on a plate and top the crisp with a dollop of whipped cream that trails down onto the plate.

1. Preheat oven to 375 degrees.

2. Mix granulated sugar, cranberries, peaches, winter savory leaves, and orange juice in a medium saucepan. Place over medium-high heat and bring just to a boil, stirring. Remove from heat and set aside.

3. In a food processor or by hand, mix oats, flour, brown sugar, and butter, pulsing in the processor or cutting up the butter with two knives until coarsely blended. Put eight 6-ounce ramekins (measuring about 3 inches across) on a parchment paper–lined baking sheet. Distribute half the oat mixture among the ramekins, patting it down slightly. Using a slotted spoon, divide the cranberry mixture among the ramekins, leaving behind excess liquid in the pan. Top with remaining oat mixture, patting it down slightly.

4. Bake 30 minutes, until topping is golden and filling is bubbly. Let cool slightly and serve, or make a few hours ahead and reheat in a 300-degree oven to serve.

8 SERVINGS

1 cup granulated sugar

1 12-ounce bag cranberries, fresh or frozen (unthawed), rinsed, picked over, and drained

8 ounces frozen (unthawed) sliced peaches (about 1¾ cups); halve each slice crosswise

1 tablespoon minced winter savory leaves

2 tablespoons orange juice

1 cup quick or old-fashioned oats

½ cup all-purpose flour

¾ cup light brown sugar

½ cup (1 stick) cold unsalted butter, cut into pieces

Cilantro Peach Cobbler

This is easily the weirdest-sounding recipe in the book, but it's actually a subtle flavor, not weird at all—until you hear the ingredients! It's based on a traditional, often sticky-sweet Southern cobbler. To peel peaches, drop them in boiling water for about 15 seconds; the skin should slip off.

½ cup (1 stick) unsalted butter

1½ tablespoons minced cilantro leaves

1¼ cups all-purpose flour

1 cup granulated sugar

⅛ teaspoon coarse salt

2 teaspoons baking powder

1 cup milk

4 cups (about 1½ pounds) peeled, sliced ripe peaches

GARNISH

Heavy cream or vanilla ice cream (optional)

1. Preheat oven to 350 degrees; put the butter in a 9-inch-square baking pan and let butter melt in the oven.

2. Whisk together cilantro leaves, flour, sugar, salt, and baking powder. Whisk in milk until smooth. Pour over melted butter; do not stir. Distribute peaches over batter.

3. Bake for 1 hour, until top is golden and set. Serve warm or at room temperature, plain or with cream or ice cream.

6 TO 8 SERVINGS

Berry-Thyme Cobbler

I wanted to do a recipe with blackberries, but they can be hard to come by and their season is short, so this recipe is flexible. You can use any baking dish that holds about 2 quarts, such as an 8-inch or 9-inch-square pan, an 11-by-7-inch pan, or a round or oval 2-quart dish. Cut the dough into circles or squares accordingly.

1. Preheat oven to 375 degrees.

2. Whisk together ½ cup sugar and cornstarch and lemon thyme leaves; gently fold in berries. Place in a 2-quart baking dish.

3. In a medium bowl, whisk together ⅓ cup sugar and the flour, baking powder, and salt. With a spatula, stir in 1¼ cups cream until a dough forms. On a lightly floured surface, pat out dough ½-inch thick. Cut into circles or squares and place on top of berries, leaving small gaps but mostly covering the surface. Re-roll scraps if needed. Brush dough with 2 tablespoons cream, then sprinkle with remaining 2 tablespoons sugar.

4. Place dish on a baking sheet to catch drips; bake cobbler 45 minutes, until berries are bubbly and biscuits are golden. Let cool slightly before serving, or serve at room temperature, with whipped cream or ice cream if desired.

4 TO 6 SERVINGS

1 cup granulated sugar, divided

1 tablespoon cornstarch

1 tablespoon minced lemon thyme leaves

3 pints blackberries, blueberries, or a mixture, rinsed, dried, and picked over

2 cups bleached all-purpose flour

1 tablespoon baking powder

½ teaspoon coarse salt

1¼ cups plus 2 tablespoons heavy cream, divided

GARNISH

Lightly Sweetened Whipped Cream (page 43) or ice cream (optional)

Bay Crème Brûlée in a Nut Crust

The delicate flavor of the bay combines well with the pecans, which give a little crunch on the bottom to go with the crisp top. I strongly prefer using a propane torch (available in hardware stores and some cookware catalogs) to caramelize the tops; you can also run them under a preheated broiler, but this runs the risk of overheating the custards. Fresh bay leaves are available in some gourmet groceries and as wreaths in gardening and cooking catalogs.

BASE

1 cup ground pecans

2 tablespoons unsalted butter, melted

2 egg whites, whisked until foamy

CUSTARD

8 fresh whole bay leaves

1½ cups heavy cream

1 cup whole or 2 percent milk

5 egg yolks

3 eggs

⅔ cup granulated sugar

½ teaspoon coarse salt

1 teaspoon vanilla extract

4 tablespoons turbinado sugar

1. Preheat the oven to 350 degrees.

2. Make base: Mix pecans and butter together and press firmly into eight 6-ounce ramekins (measuring about 3 inches across). Place the ramekins in a 9-by-13-inch pan and bake 10 minutes. Remove from oven, leaving oven on. Using a pastry brush, gently cover pecans with beaten egg whites, being sure to cover the bases completely to seal in the pecans. Return to oven for 8 minutes. Set aside; leave oven on.

3. Make custard: Snip the bay leaves into quarters with scissors into a medium saucepan; add cream and milk. Bring to a simmer over medium heat; remove from heat and pour through a strainer. In a medium bowl, whisk egg yolks, eggs, sugar, and salt together just until blended, not frothy. Pour in about ¼ cup cream mixture, whisking constantly; slowly whisk in remaining cream, trying not to create froth. Stir in vanilla. Divide custard among ramekins, straining it first if needed to remove yolk clumps.

4. Fill a pitcher with hot tap water. Place baking pan in oven and pour in water to come halfway up sides of the ramekins. Bake for

35 to 45 minutes, until centers are set and a skewer inserted into the middle of a custard comes out nearly clean. Remove from water and let cool at room temperature 30 minutes; chill, covered, at least 3 hours, until very cold.

5. To serve, sprinkle turbinado sugar evenly over custards and heat with a propane torch just until sugar caramelizes. Serve immediately, or chill up to 1 day; serve cold.

8 SERVINGS

Cherry-Lavender Clafouti

With flavors to remind you of France, this eggy, thick fruit pancake makes a super-easy and interesting dessert; not many people know what a clafouti is. And just saying the word will make kids laugh and try it.

1 pound (about 2 cups) pitted sweet cherries, fresh or frozen, thawed and drained

4 eggs

⅔ cup granulated sugar

1 cup milk, preferably whole or 2 percent

2 teaspoons vanilla extract

¾ cup all-purpose flour

⅛ teaspoon coarse salt

¾ teaspoon dried lavender flowers

GARNISH

Confectioners' sugar

1. Preheat oven to 350 degrees; butter a 9- or 10-inch pie plate.

2. Place cherries in pie plate. Whirl eggs, sugar, milk, vanilla, flour, salt, and lavender flowers in a blender just until mixed (or whisk thoroughly by hand). Pour over cherries and bake 45 to 55 minutes, until puffed and golden and a tester inserted in the middle comes out clean. Let cool 10 to 15 minutes, dust with confectioners' sugar, and serve.

6 TO 8 SERVINGS

Marjoram Papaya Fool

I prepared myself for the inevitable "I must be a fool to eat this" comments when I tested this recipe on friends, but, strange though it sounds, the marjoram really works here and actually makes a very mild-flavored dessert. (A fool is just an old-fashioned dessert of pureed fruit folded into whipped cream.) Papayas are ripe when yellow and soft; they usually need to finish ripening after purchase.

1. Slice papayas in half and discard seeds. Scoop out flesh and place in a blender or food processor with marjoram, orange juice, and lemon juice. Puree until papayas are smooth and marjoram is finely chopped.

2. In a medium bowl, whip cream on high until soft peaks form; beat in sugar. Gently fold papaya puree into cream; spoon into serving dishes or wine glasses. Serve immediately, or chill up to 4 hours.

4 SERVINGS

2 ripe papayas

1 tablespoon (packed) whole marjoram leaves

2 tablespoons orange juice

2 tablespoons fresh lemon juice

1 cup plus 2 tablespoons heavy cream

⅓ cup confectioners' sugar

Chocolate–Orange Mint Mousse

Recipes for chocolate mousse often call for both raw egg whites and yolks. I don't like risking

death by salmonella (or even stomachache by salmonella) just for a little chocolate, so I skip

the yolks and use powdered egg whites (I use Just Whites brand). If you trust your eggs,

substitute 3 egg whites at room temperature for the powdered whites and 6 tablespoons water.

8 ounces semisweet or bittersweet chocolate, chopped (or use good-quality chocolate chips)

2 ounces unsweetened chocolate, chopped

¼ cup orange juice

2 teaspoons orange liqueur, such as Grand Marnier

2 tablespoons minced orange mint leaves

2 tablespoons powdered egg whites

6 tablespoons warm water

Pinch of cream of tartar

Pinch of coarse salt

¼ cup granulated sugar

1 cup whipping cream

GARNISH

Glazed Oranges (recipe follows) or one half recipe for Orange Compote (see page 44)

1. In a double boiler set over barely simmering water, melt both chocolates. Whisk in orange juice, liqueur, and mint leaves until smooth; transfer to a large mixing bowl and set aside.

2. In a copper, stainless steel, or glass mixing bowl, whisk together powdered egg whites and warm water until powder is dissolved. Add cream of tartar and salt and continue whisking by hand or with an electric mixer until soft peaks form. Gradually whisk in sugar until stiff peaks form (this may take longer than you're accustomed to with fresh egg whites).

3. In another bowl, beat cream until it holds soft peaks.

4. Take a whiskful of egg whites and whisk into chocolate mixture. Then gently fold in remaining whites with a spatula. When whites are almost incorporated, gently fold in cream. Chill at least 30 minutes before serving.

5. Serve mousse in wine glasses or in dollops on dessert plates, surrounded by Glazed Oranges or Orange Compote.

6 SERVINGS

Glazed Oranges

I learned this simple but impressive technique from the book *The Professional Pastry Chef*; it makes a spectacular garnish for the mousse. You'll need a candy thermometer to make it.

1. Pierce each orange segment with a wooden or metal skewer and set aside (you'll hold the skewer for dipping). Spray a baking sheet with spray oil or coat it with vegetable oil and set next to oranges. Set a heatproof bowl large enough to hold the base of a large saucepan next to the stove and fill it halfway with cold water.

2. In the saucepan over medium heat, bring sugar and water to a boil, whisking. When it comes to a simmer, whisk in corn syrup. *From this point, do not stir again.* Return to a boil; cover and cook for 3 to 5 minutes, so the steam will remove sugar clinging to the sides. Uncover and let cook until mixture reaches 310 degrees. Immediately remove from heat and plunge base of saucepan into bowl of water to stop the cooking—do not let water get into the sugar syrup.

3. Working quickly, dip each orange segment into the syrup, twirling to let as much syrup drip off as possible—you want a very thin coat. Set on oiled sheet to cool. These will keep only for a few hours before the orange juice softens the crisp glaze, so don't make too far ahead.

3 or 4 seedless oranges, peeled and pulled apart into segments, white pith removed as much as possible

3 cups granulated sugar

½ cup water

⅓ cup corn syrup

Cranberry–Cinnamon Basil Rice Pudding

So you think you hate rice pudding? This easy recipe may convert you; it's certainly converted many friends of mine. It's luxuriously creamy and rich, even when made with 2 percent or skim milk.

1 ½ cups heavy cream

1 ½ cups milk

1 tablespoon unsalted butter

½ cup arborio or medium-grain rice

⅓ cup granulated sugar

½ teaspoon coarse salt

2 tablespoons minced cinnamon basil leaves

¾ cup dried cranberries

1 teaspoon vanilla extract

GARNISH

Cinnamon basil leaves

1. Preheat oven to 325 degrees; butter a 2-quart or larger baking dish.

2. Whisk together cream, milk, butter (not melted—it will melt in baking), rice, sugar, and salt. Pour into prepared dish. Cover and bake 40 minutes.

3. Remove from oven and stir in cinnamon basil leaves and cranberries. Replace cover and bake 25 to 30 minutes more; the pudding should be slightly saucy and the rice barely chewy; it will thicken upon standing.

4. Stir in vanilla and let stand 5 minutes before serving.

4 TO 6 SERVINGS

Apricot-Rosemary Rice Pudding

After trying this recipe (and others) using dried apricots, I have concluded that I simply dislike dried apricots. But I love apricot flavor, so this is my compromise—and a pretty pleasant one.

1. Preheat oven to 325 degrees; butter a 2-quart or larger baking dish.

2. Whisk together cream, milk, butter (not melted—it will melt in baking), rice, sugar, and salt. Pour into prepared dish.

3. Cover and bake 30 minutes. Stir and submerge rosemary sprig in the mixture (preferably tied in cheesecloth or a coffee filter, so you don't end up with rosemary leaves floating around). Cover and bake 35 to 40 minutes more. The pudding should be slightly saucy and the rice barely chewy; it will thicken upon standing.

4. Remove rosemary; stir in jam and vanilla, and let stand 5 minutes before serving.

4 TO 6 SERVINGS

1 ½ cups heavy cream

1 ½ cups milk

1 tablespoon unsalted butter

½ cup arborio or medium-grain rice

¼ cup granulated sugar

½ teaspoon coarse salt

3-inch sprig rosemary

½ cup all-fruit apricot jam

½ teaspoon vanilla extract

Chocolate-Lime Bread Pudding

Lime (unlike lemon) goes fabulously with chocolate and here makes a simple but rewarding pudding. I've made this pudding with skim milk and still found it rich and satisfying, for those times when I need a lower-fat chocolate indulgence. You can use brioche, challah, or French bread; if your bread is fresh, cut it up and leave it out for about 30 minutes to dry slightly.

3 cups milk

4 eggs

1¼ cups granulated sugar

⅓ cup unsweetened cocoa powder

½ teaspoon coarse salt

3 tablespoons minced lime basil leaves

2 teaspoons vanilla extract

2½ cups day-old bread cubes (cut in ½-inch cubes)

GARNISH

Lime basil leaves; Lightly Sweetened Whipped Cream (page 43), optional

1. Preheat oven to 350 degrees. Grease a 7-by-11-inch baking pan.

2. Heat milk in a small saucepan just until steaming. In a large bowl, whisk together eggs, sugar, cocoa powder, salt, lime basil leaves, and vanilla. Very slowly whisk in hot milk. Fold in bread cubes; pour mixture into prepared baking pan.

3. Fill a small pitcher with hot water. Put baking pan into a 9-by-13-inch or similar size pan and place in oven; pour in hot water to come ⅓ up the side of the 7-by-11 pan.

4. Bake 60 to 75 minutes, until pudding is just set. Serve warm, plain or with whipped cream.

6 SERVINGS

Rosemary Apple Strudel

I love desserts that use phyllo, since I love anything crisp. If you can find fresh phyllo, use it—it's much easier to handle.

1. Preheat oven to 375 degrees.

2. Spread walnuts on a baking sheet and toast in oven 7 minutes. Remove and let cool; leave oven on.

3. Mix apples with walnuts, ¾ cup sugar, 1 tablespoon melted butter, and the rosemary leaves.

4. Unroll phyllo and place 1 sheet on a work surface; keep remaining sheets covered with a damp towel. Brush sheet lightly with some of the remaining butter and sprinkle with about 2 teaspoons sugar. Cover with another sheet of phyllo; repeat the brushing and sprinkling. Continue until all phyllo sheets are stacked, buttering and sugaring the top layer as well.

5. With one of the long sides facing you, spread apple mixture lengthwise over the bottom third of the phyllo, leaving ½ inch bare at the short edges. Fold in the short edges, then roll up from the long side, jelly-roll style. Place seam side down on a parchment paper–lined baking sheet; brush top lightly with remaining butter and sprinkle with remaining sugar.

6. Bake strudel 35 minutes, or until golden and crisp. Serve warm, sliced on the diagonal, either plain or with a scoop of ice cream. This is best served the day it's made; if you hold it overnight, recrisp it in a 350-degree oven for 5 to 10 minutes.

½ cup chopped walnuts

3 medium baking apples (such as Granny Smiths), peeled, cut into ¼-inch chunks

¾ cup plus 5 tablespoons granulated sugar, divided

5 tablespoons unsalted butter, melted, divided

1 ½ teaspoons minced rosemary leaves

6 sheets phyllo, thawed if frozen

GARNISH

Vanilla ice cream (optional)

6 SERVINGS

Thyme-Roasted Plums

This is the recipe without a home—it doesn't quite fit in any of these chapters, but it probably

works best here. These plums are quick to prepare, can keep one week in the refrigerator, and

can make a low-fat dessert when eaten straight or with angel food cake. The syrup keeps them

from seeming so low-fat.

1 cup water

½ cup granulated sugar

2 tablespoons minced
  thyme leaves

2 tablespoons orange
  juice

1½ pounds red plums
  (about 10), halved
  and pitted

Dash fresh lemon juice
  (optional)

GARNISH

Ice cream, angel food
  cake, or pound cake
  (optional)

1. Preheat oven to 450 degrees (425 degrees if using a glass pan).

2. Bring water, sugar, thyme leaves, and orange juice to a boil in a small saucepan. Pour over plums that are arranged skin-side up in a 9-inch-square baking pan or other pan just large enough to hold the plums in one layer.

3. Bake 25 minutes, until plums are tender (skins may split). Pour liquid from pan back into saucepan and boil until reduced to a thin syrup, about 5 minutes. Meanwhile, wipe off excess thyme leaves from plums and discard. Pour syrup through a strainer over plums and let cool slightly before serving; taste syrup and add lemon juice if needed to balance sweetness.

4. Serve warm, plain, over ice cream, or alongside cake.

4 SERVINGS

Frozen

Desserts

Banana Mint Ice Cream

Just about the easiest ice cream you can make; stick the bananas in the freezer in the morning and make ice cream that night in about 3 minutes in a food processor. Not all flavored mints live up to their name, but banana mint does, to my surprise. You can make this with regular mint, but it's worth seeking out the banana version.

1. Put the banana slices in a single layer on a baking sheet lined with parchment or waxed paper and freeze until solid, about 2 hours.

2. Transfer the slices to a food processor bowl; add sour cream, heavy cream, confectioners' sugar, and mint leaves. Process until ice cream is smooth and thick. Serve immediately as a soft-serve ice cream, or store in freezer.

ABOUT 1 PINT

5 medium, very ripe bananas (about 2 pounds), peeled and cut into ½-inch slices

½ cup sour cream

¾ cup heavy cream

⅓ cup confectioners' sugar

2 teaspoons minced banana mint leaves

Lemon-Blueberry Sorbet

Like the Banana Mint Ice Cream, this is one of the easiest frozen desserts to make, taking full advantage of frozen fruits and a food processor. It's especially satisfying to eat knowing there's no fat in it.

⅔ cup granulated sugar

⅓ cup whole lemon verbena leaves

1 bag frozen blueberries (14 to 16 ounces)

⅓ cup fresh lemon juice

2 tablespoons lemon-flavored rum (optional)

Put sugar and lemon verbena leaves in a food processor and process 30 seconds. Add frozen berries and process 1 minute. With the processor on, pour lemon juice and rum, if using, through the feed tube; process until smooth. Serve immediately, or transfer to a covered bowl and keep in freezer (soften slightly before serving, if necessary).

4 SERVINGS

Cinnamon Basil Ice Cream

This is as easy as churned ice cream gets. Like all ice creams made without eggs, it's a soft-serve style that melts quickly right out of the ice cream maker; if you have time, keep it in the freezer for a few hours before serving. I like the pretty green flecks of basil, but if you want your ice cream totally smooth, follow these steps instead: Combine the cream, milk, and basil in a saucepan and bring just to a simmer. Remove from heat, cover, and set aside to steep for 10 minutes. Strain, add remaining ingredients, and refrigerate until cold, then freeze in your ice cream maker.

1. Whisk all ingredients together until sugar is dissolved. Freeze according to your ice cream maker's directions. Serve immediately or store in freezer.

ABOUT 1 QUART

2 cups heavy cream

1 cup whole or 2 percent milk

½ cup granulated sugar, preferably superfine

2 tablespoons finely minced cinnamon basil leaves

1 teaspoon ground cinnamon

Cinnamon Basil–Apple Ice Cream

Great on its own, this ice cream takes the Apple–Basil Cake on page 39 to decadent heights.

1 tablespoon unsalted butter

2 medium cooking apples, such as Granny Smiths, peeled and coarsely chopped

½ cup granulated sugar

1 teaspoon ground cinnamon

2 cups heavy cream

1 cup whole or 2 percent milk

2 tablespoons finely minced cinnamon basil leaves

1. In a medium skillet over medium-high heat, melt butter. Add apples and sauté about 3 minutes, until apples just begin to soften. Mix in sugar and cinnamon and sauté 3 to 5 minutes more, until apples are lightly caramelized and syrupy. Remove from heat, transfer to ice cream canister, and chill in freezer 15 minutes.

2. Whisk in cream, milk, and cinnamon basil leaves. Freeze according to your ice cream maker's directions. Serve immediately or store in freezer.

ABOUT 1 QUART

Peppermint Ice Cream with Mint Julep Truffles

Strongly minty (though with real mint, it may not taste like the peppermint-candy ice cream you're used to) and dotted with creamy truffles, this ice cream is interesting and elegant enough for a party; serve it with extra whole truffles on the side.

1. In a medium saucepan, mix cream, milk, and mint leaves; bring just to a simmer over medium-high heat. Remove from heat, cover and let stand 5 minutes. Strain into a bowl.

2. In a medium saucepan, whisk together yolks and sugar; very gradually whisk in hot cream mixture. Cook over medium-low heat, whisking, until mixture is thick enough to coat the back of a spoon, about 8 to 10 minutes. Pour into ice cream canister and chill in freezer 30 to 45 minutes, until cold, stirring every 15 minutes.

3. Freeze according to your ice cream maker's directions; just before ice cream is solid, mix in truffles. Serve immediately or store in freezer.

ABOUT 1 QUART

2 cups heavy cream

1 cup whole or 2 percent milk

1 tablespoon minced mint leaves

4 egg yolks

½ cup granulated sugar

12 Mint Julep Truffles (page 15), each cut into 8 pieces and frozen while you prepare ice cream

Fennel Lemon Buttermilk Sorbet

This simple, refreshing sorbet tastes much richer than it is, thanks to the buttermilk. You can

replace the fennel with tarragon, if you prefer.

4 cups (1 quart) nonfat
or low-fat buttermilk

3 tablespoons fresh
lemon juice

¾ cup granulated sugar

2 tablespoons minced
fennel leaves

1. In an ice cream canister, whisk all ingredients together until sugar is dissolved. Freeze according to your ice cream maker's directions (sorbet will be slightly soft). Serve immediately or store in freezer.

ABOUT 1 QUART

Pine Nut–Lavender Brittle Ice Cream

Because this is so rich, smooth, and sweet, small scoops will go a long way. Aim for somewhere between a coarse and a fine chop on the brittle, discarding any brittle powder created during the chopping.

1. In a small saucepan, bring honey and lavender to a simmer over medium heat. Pour through a strainer into a medium bowl and cool slightly.

2. In a medium saucepan, bring milk and cream just to a simmer. Meanwhile, whisk together cooled honey, egg yolks, and salt; slowly whisk in ¼ cup of the hot milk mixture. Whisk egg mixture into remaining milk in saucepan. Cook over medium-low heat, whisking, until mixture is thick enough to coat the back of a spoon, about 8 to 10 minutes.

3. Pour into ice cream canister and chill in freezer 30 to 45 minutes until cold, stirring every 15 minutes. Freeze according to your ice cream maker's directions; just before ice cream is solid, mix in brittle. Serve immediately or store in freezer.

ABOUT I QUART

⅔ cup honey

2 teaspoons dried
    lavender flowers

1 cup whole or 2
    percent milk

2 cups heavy cream

4 egg yolks

¼ teaspoon coarse salt

2 cups chopped Pine
    Nut–Lavender Brittle
    (page 18)

Pineapple Sage—Buttermilk Sherbet

Quick, easy, low-fat, and refreshing in summer, this is a perfect way to use some of the

pineapple sage that grows into a bush by midsummer.

1 quart nonfat or low-fat buttermilk

1 cup whole or 2 percent milk

1 cup granulated sugar

¼ teaspoon coarse salt

¼ cup minced pineapple sage leaves

2 8-ounce cans crushed pineapple (or 1 15-ounce can), packed in juice, drained

1. In the canister of your ice cream maker, whisk together buttermilk, milk, sugar, salt, and pineapple sage leaves until sugar is dissolved. Stir in pineapple. Freeze according to your ice cream maker's directions. Serve immediately or store in freezer.

ABOUT 1½ QUARTS

Frozen Double-Lemon Soufflés

I love how light and smooth these are, and they're quite easy—don't let making the meringue scare you. You will need an inexpensive instant-read thermometer for the meringue.

1. Put four 6-ounce ramekins (measuring about 3 inches across) on a baking sheet.

2. Grind sugar and lemon thyme and lemon verbena leaves in a food processor for 15 seconds, until herbs are finely ground. In a large, heatproof mixing bowl, whisk together sugar mixture and egg whites. Set over a pan of simmering water—bottom of bowl should not touch water. Whisk constantly until whites reach 140 degrees.

3. Immediately remove from heat, add cream of tartar, and beat with a mixer on medium speed until stiff and cool to the touch (both meringue and bowl should feel cool). Set aside.

4. In another bowl, whip cream until it forms soft peaks. Beat in lemon juice, beating until cream is stiff. Fold cream into beaten egg whites, gently but thoroughly. Divide among ramekins, mounding each slightly. Freeze until firm.

5. To serve, set ramekins on dessert plates, and let soufflés thaw about 5 minutes. Garnish with herb sprigs.

4 SERVINGS

½ cup granulated sugar

1 tablespoon (packed) whole lemon thyme leaves

1 tablespoon (packed) whole lemon verbena leaves

4 egg whites

Pinch cream of tartar

¾ cup heavy cream

3 tablespoons fresh lemon juice

GARNISH

Lemon thyme or lemon verbena sprigs

Plated

Desserts

Basiled Peaches Bruschetta with Pineapple Mint Custard Sauce

This is definitely a rustic dessert, but it's an awfully pretty rustic. If you can't find challah or brioche, you could use pound cake instead, but omit the sugar in the peaches if you do.

1. Make sauce: In a small saucepan, whisk together mint leaves and milk; heat over medium heat until milk begins to steam. Whisk together yolks and sugar in a small bowl. Very slowly whisk in hot milk; return mixture to saucepan. Cook, whisking constantly, over medium-low heat until sauce thickens just enough to coat the back of a spoon. Do not boil. Pour through a strainer into a small pitcher or measuring cup. Chill if not using immediately.

2. Toss peaches, basil leaves, and sugar together.

3. To serve, pour a little sauce onto 4 dessert plates. Top with challah slices and divide peach mixture over slices. Drizzle with a little more sauce; garnish plates with herb leaves and serve.

4 SERVINGS

PINEAPPLE MINT CUSTARD SAUCE

3 tablespoons minced pineapple mint leaves

1¼ cups half-and-half or whole milk

3 egg yolks

⅓ cup granulated sugar

BRUSCHETTA

2 ripe peaches, sliced

5 teaspoons minced basil leaves

1 tablespoon granulated sugar

4 1-inch-thick slices challah or brioche, toasted until outside is crisp

GARNISH

Basil and pineapple mint leaves

Seckel Pear Purses with Lemon Balm—Almond Filling

This dessert is surprisingly easy, given how impressive it looks. Be sure to have extra lemon balm leaves on hand for garnish, to brighten the plate.

1 cup sliced almonds

¼ cup granulated sugar

¼ cup loosely packed whole lemon balm leaves

1 egg

1 tablespoon unsalted butter, softened

½ teaspoon almond extract

12 firm-ripe seckel pears

6 sheets fresh or frozen, thawed phyllo (keep covered until ready to use)

2 tablespoons unsalted butter, melted

SAUCE

1 cup granulated sugar

2 tablespoons water

1 tablespoon fresh lemon juice

⅓ cup heavy cream

1 tablespoon unsalted butter

(Continued)

1. Preheat oven to 375 degrees.

2. Finely grind almonds and sugar in a food processor. Add lemon balm leaves, egg, butter, and almond extract, and process until leaves are ground.

3. With an apple corer or paring knife, core pears, working from the bottom up and leaving stem and flesh intact. If pears cannot stand up, cut a thin slice off the bottom. Fill each cavity with about 2 teaspoons almond filling.

4. Cut phyllo sheets in half to make twelve 14-by-9-inch pieces. Work with 1 piece at a time; keep remaining sheets covered. Brush a sheet lightly with melted butter and place a pear in the center. Gather the phyllo up around the pear, folding back the top so the stem shows. Brush top lightly with butter. Set on a parchment paper–lined baking sheet. Repeat with remaining pears. Bake pears for 10 to 12 minutes, until phyllo is golden and crisp.

5. Meanwhile, prepare sauce: In a medium saucepan, whisk together sugar, water, and lemon juice. Bring to a boil without stirring, brushing down sides once with a pastry brush dipped in water. Cook until the sugar turns golden around the edge of the

pan, then swirl the pan continuously until the sauce is a deep golden caramel (this takes 5 to 10 minutes). Remove from the heat and carefully pour in cream; sauce will sputter and bubble up. Stir in butter and whisk until smooth, returning to low heat if needed.

6. To serve: Ladle a circle of sauce onto each plate. Top with 2 pear purses and drizzle with a little more caramel. Garnish with lemon balm leaves. Serve warm.

6 SERVINGS

GARNISH

Lemon balm leaves or sprigs

White Chocolate—Lavender Napoleons

This is a great do-ahead (completely, even to the plating) dessert for a party. It won't be as pretty if you don't have a pastry bag, but you can just garnish with dollops of whipped cream.

8 ounces good-quality white chocolate, broken up

1 teaspoon dried lavender flowers, divided

3 tablespoons granulated sugar

1 tablespoon all-purpose flour

1 tablespoon cornstarch

Pinch of coarse salt

¾ cup milk

2 eggs

1 teaspoon vanilla extract

1 tablespoon unsalted butter

1½ cups heavy cream

2 tablespoons confectioners' sugar

⅔ cup blueberry preserves

½ pint fresh blueberries

1. Melt the white chocolate in a double boiler set over, not touching, barely simmering water, stirring until smooth. Cover a baking sheet with parchment paper and spread melted chocolate as evenly as possible into two 14-by-5-inch strips. Sprinkle 1 strip with ½ teaspoon lavender, slightly crumbling it. Cover strips with another piece of parchment paper, pressing slightly to embed the lavender. Chill until firm, at least 1 hour.

2. Meanwhile, prepare pastry cream: In a medium saucepan, whisk together sugar, flour, cornstarch, and salt. Whisk in milk, then eggs. Set over medium-low heat and cook, whisking, until mixture comes to a full boil. Remove from heat and whisk in vanilla and butter until melted; pastry cream will be quite thick. Pour into a medium bowl (straining it if you see pieces of cooked egg), press plastic wrap directly onto surface, and chill at least 1 hour until cold.

3. To assemble napoleons: Whip the cream to stiff peaks, adding confectioners' sugar after it has just begun to stiffen. Fold half of the whipped cream into the chilled pastry cream; put remaining whipped cream in a pastry bag with a star tip. Stir preserves and remaining ½ teaspoon lavender together. Working quickly (chocolate softens fast), break each chilled chocolate strip

crosswise into 6 jagged but similar-size rectangles, setting aside 4 of the lavender-topped rectangles. Place 1 rectangle on each of 4 serving plates. Spread with a thin layer of preserves, then top with a layer of pastry cream. Press in 8 blueberries. Top with another chocolate rectangle and repeat. Top with lavender-topped rectangles, lavender side up. Pipe whipped cream in a swirl onto each napoleon, and pipe cream rosettes around plate. Top rosettes with berries and sprinkle plate lightly with more lavender, if desired. Chill or serve immediately; can be made up to 1 day ahead.

4 SERVINGS

Coeurs à la Crème with Raspberry-Mint Sauce

You have two options here, full-fat and reduced-fat. Either way, these cool and creamy hearts, which require no cooking, make a great summer dessert. If you don't have individual molds, or one large one, line a round colander with dampened cheesecloth instead; when you turn it out, you'll have a nice dome to cut into wedges.

8 ounces cream cheese (do not use reduced-fat), softened, *or* 16 ounces low-fat or nonfat vanilla yogurt

⅔ cup confectioners' sugar

1½ teaspoons vanilla extract

1 cup heavy cream

SAUCE

1 12-ounce bag frozen raspberries

2 tablespoons granulated sugar

¼ cup (packed) whole mint leaves

GARNISH

Mint leaves

1. *If using cream cheese:* In a medium bowl, beat cream cheese, sugar, and vanilla until smooth. In a separate bowl with clean beaters, beat cream until it just forms stiff peaks. Fold into cream cheese mixture, then follow directions in Step 2 for placing in molds.

If using yogurt: Place the yogurt in a fine-mesh strainer lined with cheesecloth or a paper towel; cover and place over a bowl. Let drain in refrigerator for at least 2 hours. Gently mix yogurt with sugar and vanilla until smooth. In a separate bowl, beat cream until it just forms stiff peaks. Fold into yogurt mixture, then follow directions in Step 2 for placing in molds.

2. To mold: Line 6 individual coeur à la crème molds with a double layer of dampened cheesecloth that hangs 1 inch over the edge. Fill to the tops; smooth tops and fold cheesecloth over. Place on a cookie sheet with a rim to catch the draining liquid. Chill 4 to 24 hours.

3. Make sauce: Puree raspberries, sugar, and mint leaves in a food processor. Press through a sieve to remove seeds.

4. To serve, put a large spoonful of sauce onto the center of 6 dessert plates. Pull back cheesecloth and invert molds over sauce and remove cheesecloth. Garnish with mint leaves; serve remaining sauce on the side.

6 SERVINGS

Peppermint Ice Cream Profiteroles with Chocolate-Mint Sauce

If you're looking for a quick recipe, you'll need to turn to other recipes in this book. While this isn't quick, it can be done in stages, and it impresses people who have never made anything with cream puffs.

PROFITEROLES

1 cup milk

½ cup (1 stick) unsalted butter

¾ teaspoon coarse salt

1 tablespoon granulated sugar

1 cup all-purpose flour

4 eggs

2 teaspoons vanilla extract

SAUCE

½ cup half-and-half or light cream

2 tablespoons unsalted butter

2 teaspoons minced mint leaves

¾ cup semisweet chocolate chips

1 teaspoon vanilla extract

(Continued)

1. Preheat oven to 400 degrees.

2. In a medium saucepan, bring milk, butter, salt, and sugar to a boil over medium heat. Immediately dump in flour and stir vigorously with a wooden spoon until mixture forms a ball and pulls away from the sides of the pan. Remove from heat.

3. With the spoon, beat in eggs 1 at a time, thoroughly incorporating each egg before adding the next. Add the vanilla with the final egg and beat until smooth.

4. With a pastry bag with a plain tip, a small ice cream scoop, or a spoon, drop 1½-inch balls of dough onto 2 parchment paper–lined baking sheets, spacing the balls 2 inches apart (you'll need at least 24 balls). Smooth down the tops as needed with a wet finger.

5. Bake the profiteroles for 15 minutes, then reverse baking sheets from top to bottom and front to back in the oven. Lower heat to 375 degrees, and bake for 20 minutes more, or until dry and crisp. Remove to a wire rack and cool.

6. Make sauce: In a small saucepan, bring half-and-half, butter, and mint leaves to a boil. Off heat, whisk in chocolate chips and vanilla until smooth. Pour sauce through a strainer to remove mint. Chill if not using shortly (if sauce gets too thick, reheat it over low heat, stirring).

7. To serve: Spoon a small amount of warm sauce onto each plate. Split open each profiterole horizontally, leaving the cap barely attached, and place 3 profiteroles on each plate. Fill with ice cream and replace caps. Drizzle with a little more sauce, dust the plate with confectioners' sugar, and garnish with mint leaves.

8 SERVINGS

FILLING

1 recipe Peppermint Ice
Cream with Mint
Julep Truffles
(page 101)

GARNISH

Confectioners' sugar,
mint leaves

Panna Cotta with Chocolate-Lavender Sauce

After crème brûlée showed up on every menu, chefs turned to panna cotta (a "cooked cream" custard) for something new. I'd been making it since a trip to Italy, where I ordered it every chance I got. I'm giving you two panna cotta recipes because it's so easy and good—people seem to feel coddled and comforted after they eat it.

PANNA COTTA

1 teaspoon unflavored gelatin

2 tablespoons cold water

1½ cups heavy cream

2 tablespoons granulated sugar

1 teaspoon vanilla extract

SAUCE

¼ cup half-and-half or light cream

1 tablespoon unsalted butter

¾ teaspoon dried lavender flowers

½ cup semisweet chocolate chips

½ teaspoon vanilla extract

1. Rinse four 6-ounce ramekins (measuring about 3 inches across) with cold water; drain but do not dry them. Set aside in a small baking pan.

2. Make panna cotta: In a small bowl, sprinkle gelatin over cold water and set aside. In a medium saucepan, whisk together cream, sugar, and vanilla. Over medium heat, bring to a simmer and let simmer slowly, stirring occasionally, for 2 minutes. Remove from heat and gently whisk in softened gelatin until dissolved (try to avoid making too much foam). Divide among ramekins; cover loosely and chill 4 to 24 hours.

3. Make sauce: In a small saucepan bring half-and-half, butter, and lavender to a boil. Off heat, whisk in chocolate chips and vanilla until smooth. Pour sauce through a strainer to remove lavender. Chill if not using shortly (if sauce gets too thick, reheat it over low heat, stirring).

4. To serve, spoon a small amount of warm sauce onto each of 4 dessert plates. Run a thin knife around the inside rim of the ramekins and invert panna cotta over sauce. Drizzle with remaining sauce.

4 SERVINGS

Coffee Panna Cotta with Anise Sauce

The flavor of the anise hyssop comes through very lightly, so as not to overwhelm the other flavors.

PANNA COTTA

1 envelope (2 teaspoons) unflavored gelatin

2 tablespoons cold water

1½ cups heavy cream

¾ cup whole milk or half-and-half

⅓ cup granulated sugar

1 teaspoon vanilla extract

2 teaspoons instant espresso powder

1 tablespoon coffee-flavored liqueur (optional)

SAUCE

¼ cup half-and-half or light cream

1 tablespoon unsalted butter

1 tablespoon minced anise hyssop leaves

½ cup semisweet chocolate chips

½ teaspoon vanilla extract

1. Rinse four 6-ounce ramekins (measuring about 3 inches across) with cold water; drain but do not dry them. Set aside in a small baking pan.

2. Make panna cotta: In a small bowl, sprinkle gelatin over cold water and set aside. In a medium saucepan, whisk together cream, milk, sugar, and vanilla. Over medium heat, bring to a simmer and let simmer slowly, stirring occasionally, for 2 minutes. Remove from heat and gently whisk in softened gelatin, espresso powder, and liqueur until dissolved (try to avoid making too much foam). Divide among ramekins; cover loosely and chill 4 to 24 hours.

3. Make sauce: In a small saucepan bring half-and-half, butter, and anise hyssop leaves to a boil. Off heat, whisk in chocolate chips and vanilla until smooth. Pour sauce through a strainer to remove anise hyssop. Chill if not using shortly (if sauce gets too thick, reheat it over low heat, stirring).

4. To serve, spoon a small amount of warm sauce onto each of 4 dessert plates. Run a thin knife around the inside rim of the ramekins and invert panna cotta over sauce. Drizzle with remaining sauce.

4 SERVINGS

Thyme- and Wine-Poached Pears

I'm including two recipes for poached pears since they're so easy and luscious—they're one of the few desserts to really appeal to me when I need something low-fat. They're nice served with biscotti for a little crunch.

1. In a large saucepan, stir together water, wine, sugar, and thyme leaves. Bring to a simmer.

2. Meanwhile, peel pears. Working from the bottom, insert an apple corer or melon baller to remove core, leaving stem intact.

3. Place pears in wine mixture; add water if needed to nearly cover the pears. Cook, uncovered, at a steady simmer. Cooking time may be anywhere from 8 minutes to 40 minutes, depending on the pears' ripeness; pears are done when they are tender and a paring knife can be inserted easily.

4. Using a slotted spoon, remove pears to small serving plates. Bring liquid in saucepan to a full boil until reduced to a thin syrup (don't let it get too thick); this may take 20 to 30 minutes. Pour through a strainer over pears.

5. Serve pears garnished with thyme sprigs; drizzle with a little cream if desired.

4 SERVINGS

4 cups water

2 cups dry red wine

¾ cup granulated sugar

¼ cup minced thyme leaves

4 pears, preferably Bosc or d'Anjou

GARNISH

Thyme sprigs; heavy cream, optional

Poached Pears with Sage-Honey Glaze

Shiny and sweet, I like these pears at least as much as the previous recipe. They cook a little faster because they're halved.

6 cups water

¾ cup granulated sugar

1 tablespoon fresh
    lemon juice

4 pears, preferably
    Bosc or d'Anjou

⅓ cup honey

2 tablespoons chopped
    sage leaves

GARNISH

Sage leaves; heavy
    cream, optional

1. In a Dutch oven or large saucepan, stir together water, sugar, and lemon juice. Bring to a simmer.

2. Meanwhile, peel pears and halve them, leaving the stem intact on one half. Working from the bottom, insert an apple corer or melon baller to remove cores.

3. Gently place pears in sugar syrup and cook, uncovered, at a steady simmer. Cooking time may be anywhere from 8 minutes to 30 minutes, depending on the pears' ripeness; pears are done when they are tender and a paring knife can be inserted easily.

4. Meanwhile, combine honey and sage leaves in a small saucepan and bring just to a simmer over medium-low heat. Remove from heat and let stand until pears are done.

5. When pears are done, remove them with a slotted spoon, draining them well, to a large plate, flat sides down. Reheat sage honey if needed to make it liquid enough to brush onto pears; strain out sage leaves. Brush honey over each pear (don't brush the flat sides). Arrange on serving plates with the stem half of each pear propped up on the other half.

6. Serve pears garnished with sage leaves; drizzle with a little cream if desired.

4 SERVINGS

Chocolate-Pistachio Terrine

This isn't one of the quickest recipes here, but it's worth making for company, as it makes a fair number of servings and looks professional. Don't chop the pistachios too fine; if you have a toaster oven, use it to toast them. You'll need an inexpensive instant-read thermometer for this recipe.

1 cup coarsely chopped unsalted pistachios

2 teaspoons unflavored gelatin

2 tablespoons water

12 ounces bittersweet or semisweet chocolate, chopped (or 2 cups high-quality chips)

3 tablespoons unsalted butter

¾ cup plus 2 tablespoons heavy cream, divided

⅓ cup minced cinnamon basil leaves

3 egg whites

¼ cup granulated sugar

GARNISH

Cinnamon basil sprigs; Cinnamon Basil Custard Sauce (page 40), or Lightly Sweetened Whipped Cream (page 43)

1. Preheat oven to 350 degrees.

2. Toast the pistachios for 10 minutes; remove and let cool completely. Line an 8-by-4-inch loaf pan with plastic wrap, and sprinkle ½ cup of the cooled pistachios in the bottom of the pan; set aside.

3. Sprinkle gelatin over water in a small, heatproof bowl; set aside to soften. Put chocolate, butter, 2 tablespoons cream, and cinnamon basil leaves in the top of a double boiler. Set over barely simmering water to melt chocolate, stirring often. Set aside when fully melted to cool somewhat.

4. In a large, heatproof mixing bowl, whisk together egg whites and sugar and set over same pan of simmering water—bottom of bowl should not touch water. Whisk until whites reach 140 degrees. Immediately remove bowl from heat (leaving pan of water on stove), and beat whites with a mixer on medium speed until stiff and cool to the touch. Set aside.

5. Turn pan of simmering water off but leave on stove; set bowl with gelatin in the pan of water and whisk until gelatin is dissolved (don't get hot water into bowl).

6. *Working quickly from here on,* beat ¾ cup cream in a medium bowl until soft peaks form; add gelatin and beat until stiff peaks form. Fold chocolate mixture into egg whites in 4 portions, then fold in whipped cream quickly but thoroughly. Pour into prepared loaf pan; sprinkle with remaining pistachios and cover with plastic wrap. Chill terrine at least 4 hours or until firm.

7. To serve, invert terrine onto a serving platter. Cut when still very cold into thin slices, but then let stand a while before serving as this is better eaten when the slices are only cool, not cold. Serve each slice on a dessert plate topped with a dollop of whipped cream and a basil sprig, or spoon a little custard sauce onto each plate and top with a slice of terrine and a basil sprig.

8 TO 12 SERVINGS

Savory Baked Apples Under Wraps

I think anything with puff pastry is delicious, and these pretty apples are no exception.

¼ cup chopped pecans

3 tablespoons unsalted butter, very soft

3 tablespoons firmly packed light brown sugar

1½ teaspoons minced winter savory leaves

4 medium cooking apples, such as Granny Smith

½ lemon

1 sheet frozen puff pastry, thawed (½ of a 17¼-ounce package)

1 egg, lightly beaten

GARNISH

Heavy cream or Lightly Sweetened Whipped Cream (page 43), optional

1. Preheat oven to 375 degrees.

2. Toast pecans on a baking sheet in the preheated oven for 5 to 7 minutes, until they are just fragrant. Cool 5 minutes. In a small bowl, stir together pecans, butter, sugar, and savory leaves with a spoon or spatula until blended. Set aside.

3. Peel apples. With a melon baller, core apples from the top down, leaving the base intact. Rub apples all over with the cut lemon and place on a parchment paper–lined, rimmed baking sheet (trim apple bases if they don't stand up straight). Stuff each apple with one-quarter of the pecan mixture, packing it down well.

4. On a lightly floured surface, roll out puff pastry to ⅛-inch thickness. Cut out four 5-inch squares. With a paring knife, cut remaining pastry into 16 leaf shapes. Lightly brush pastry squares with beaten egg; drape squares over apples (egg-washed side up). Top each square with 4 pastry leaves; brush these with egg.

5. Bake 45 minutes, until pastry is golden and crisp and apples are tender. Serve plain or garnished with a little cream or whipped cream.

4 SERVINGS

Chocolate-Basil Truffle Rounds

Individual desserts seem to make people feel special, so I use tartlet tins and ramekins constantly. Here the tins hold wonderfully rich, easy, and impressively dense desserts that are good—though different—both cold and at room temperature. Try them both ways to see which you prefer.

1. Preheat oven to 350 degrees; butter or grease eight 4-inch, removable-bottom tartlet tins; set tins on a baking sheet.

2. Melt butter with basil leaves in the top of a double boiler set over (not touching) barely simmering water. Add chocolate; stir often until chocolate is melted. Set aside top pan to cool slightly; mixture will be very thick.

3. In a medium bowl, beat egg whites until they form soft peaks; add sugar and beat until stiff peaks form. In a small bowl, whisk egg yolks until bubbly; whisk into chocolate mixture. Fold in about ¼ cup beaten whites to lighten the chocolate mixture, then gently but thoroughly fold in remaining whites.

4. Divide batter among tins. Bake 15 minutes, until tops have just set (mixture will still be soft in the middle). Let cool on a wire rack (the puffed tops will fall), then chill, covered, until ready to serve.

5. To serve, remove tin sides. With a thin-bladed metal spatula, lift rounds from the bases and transfer to dessert plates. Serve cold or at room temperature, with a dollop of whipped cream or a small pool of custard sauce; garnish with basil sprigs.

6 tablespoons unsalted butter

2 tablespoons minced basil leaves

¾ pound bittersweet or semisweet chocolate, chopped

3 eggs, separated

2 tablespoons sugar

GARNISH

Basil sprigs; Lightly Sweetened Whipped Cream (page 43) or Cinnamon Basil Custard Sauce (page 40); made without cinnamon stick and with sweet basil instead of cinnamon basil)

8 SERVINGS

Orange Mint Crème Caramel

Jiggly, smooth, and not too sweet, these make terrific light endings to a summer meal.

1 ½ cups granulated
  sugar, divided

⅓ cup (packed) whole
  orange mint leaves

¼ cup water

2 cups whole or 2
  percent milk

3 whole eggs

2 egg yolks

1 teaspoon vanilla
  extract

GARNISH

Orange mint sprigs

1. Preheat oven to 350 degrees. Set six 6-ounce ramekins (measuring about 3 inches across) in a 9-by-13-inch or similar size pan.

2. In a food processor or blender, grind 1 cup sugar and the mint leaves until leaves are minced. Transfer to a small saucepan or skillet and stir in the water. Cook, stirring, over medium heat until sugar dissolves. Brush down sides of pan with a pastry brush dipped in water. Continue to cook without stirring until mixture begins to turn golden; continue cooking, swirling pan, until caramel turns a deep golden color (this will take 5 to 10 minutes). Remove from heat and divide among ramekins; working quickly, swirl ramekins to coat bottoms and a little up the sides with caramel. Be careful—caramel makes a nasty burn.

3. Bring milk just a simmer in a medium saucepan. In a medium bowl, whisk together remaining ½ cup sugar and the eggs and egg yolks. Very slowly whisk in hot milk, then vanilla, whisking gently to prevent foaming. Pour through a strainer into ramekins.

4. Fill a pitcher or measuring cup with hot water. Place pan with ramekins in oven and pour in water to come halfway up the sides of ramekins. Bake 45 to 50 minutes, until a toothpick inserted in the center comes out clean but custards are still a bit jiggly. Remove ramekins from water; cool 15 minutes, and serve, or chill, covered, up to 2 days.

5. To serve, run a sharp, thin knife around the edge of the ramekins. Put a small serving plate over each ramekin and invert—the custard should fall out. Garnish with mint.

6 SERVINGS

A Few Mail-Order Sources

🌿 CATHEDRAL GREENHOUSE, AT THE WASHINGTON NATIONAL CATHEDRAL, Massachusetts and Wisconsin Avenues, NW, Washington, D.C. 20016-5098; (202) 537-6263. Carries banana mint and many other herb plants.

🌿 WELL-SWEEP HERB FARM, 205 Mt. Bethel Road, Port Murray, NJ 07865; (908) 852-5390. Carries allspice trees and a great selection of herb plants.

🌿 BAKER'S CATALOGUE, FROM KING ARTHUR'S FLOUR, (800) 827-6836. Carries parchment paper, baking sheets, and many other baking supplies.

🌿 BRIDGE KITCHENWARE, 214 E. 52nd Street, New York, NY 10022; (212) 838-6746. A restaurant supply company that also sells retail; carries parchment paper and many other baking supplies.

🌿 SWEET CELEBRATIONS, (800) 328-6722. Carries tartlet pans, madeleine pans, and many other baking supplies.

Index

C

M

Macaroons, Buttercream Filled, 22
Madeleines, Triple-Lemon, 27
Maple Walnut Cookies, 20
Marjoram, 7
    Papaya Fool, 87
Meringue:
    Chocolate Mint Meringue Torte, 70–71
    Frozen Double-Lemon Souffles, 105
Milk, 10
Mint, 7
    Blueberry-Mint Layer Cake, 48–49
    Coeurs à la Crème with Raspberry-Mint Sauce, 114–115
    Julep Truffles, 15, 101, 116–117
    Peppermint Ice Cream Profiteroles with Chocolate-Mint Sauce, 116–117
    Peppermint Ice Cream with Mint Julep Truffles, 101
Mint, Banana, 131
    Ice Cream, 97
Mint, Chocolate, 7
    Biscotti, 24

Brownie Sandwiches, 32
Buttercream, 23, 32
Buttercream-Filled Macaroons, 22
Meringue Torte, 70–71
Mint, Orange, 7
    Buttercream, 23, 32
    Buttercream-Filled Macaroons, 22
    Chocolate Mint Brownie Sandwiches, 32
    Chocolate–Orange Mint Mousse, 88
    Crème Caramel, 128–129
    Polenta Cake with Orange Compote, 44–45
    Starfruit-Mint Tartlets, 66
Mint, Pineapple, 7
    Basiled Peaches Bruschetta with Pineapple Mint Custard Sauce, 109
    Pineapple–Pineapple Mint Upside-Down Cake, 42–43
Mixed Berry Turnovers, 75
Mousse, Chocolate–Orange Mint, 88

N

Napoleons, White Chocolate–Lavender, 112–113

O

Orange(s):
    Chocolate–Orange Mint Mousse, 88
    Compote, 44–45, 88
    Glazed Oranges, 89
    Mint Buttercream, 23, 32
    Mint Polenta Cake with Orange Compote, 44–45
    Sugar Cookies, 21
    see also Mint, Orange
Orange Mint Crème Caramel, 128–129

P

Panna Cotta:
    Coffee, with Anise Sauce, 120
    with Chocolate-Lavender Sauce, 118–119
Parchment paper, 11, 131
Peach(es):

R

S